CERTIFIED

One Unexpected Birth…One Hapless Wedding…
One Bizarre Death

By

Roger Wilson-Crane

Published by New Generation Publishing in 2021

Copyright © Roger Wilson-Crane 2021

First Edition

ISBN
        Paperback   978-1-80031-109-1
        Ebook   978-1-80031-108-4

www.newgeneration-publishing.com

 New Generation Publishing

To Holly and Vic. For Being There.

One Unexpected Birth

Chapter One:

I didn't have a serious girlfriend until much later in my adult journey. Louise was probably the nearest I had in those early years. She was a nurse at the Royal Free Hospital in London. We met when we were both eighteen and I was visiting an old school friend who had ended up living in Camden Town, putting up satellite dishes for a rather suspect company. He lived in an apartment block that also housed one of the Bananarama girls, which was cool for a teenager, like me, from a Yorkshire village, whose only famous resident was Russell Harty. I am quite sure, looking back, that I was never in love with Louise, and vice versa. I think the attraction and longevity of this relationship, for me, boiled down to her being absolutely identical, in looks, to my footballing idol Peter Beardsley. Those of you who know who I mean will now be spitting out your relaxing beverage with incredulity and those that do not, make your favourite tipple, google him, and then spit...

It is amazing how memories start to flood back, and I realise I have already told you a fib. Russell Harty was not the only celebrity from our village. We also had Thelma Barlow who played Mavis for many years in Coronation Street. She was a warm, funny lady who embraced village life unlike the certain chat show host.

I was fortunate to get to know her in my teenage years as I worked in the local hotel where she was a frequent visitor. In those days, prior to meeting Peter (sorry, Louise!), I would hitch lifts via my trusty thumb to visit a girlfriend in the next village ten miles away. The girl in question was stunning, and a bit out of my league to be honest, and for some reason she never called me by my real name. I was always introduced to those she knew as Penfold. At the time, being named after Danger Mouse's reluctant sidekick was quite endearing, but looking back now, she was obviously taking the proverbial. Anyway, I was on the main road, frozen thumb in the air, waiting for someone to take pity on me, when a car stopped to pick me up. It was a small funky looking car, bright yellow, that stood out even in the gloom. I could just make out three passengers through the fading light. As the window wound down, Thelma's head popped out.

"Hello, where are you heading?" she asked, cheerily.

"Hi! I am just popping over to Ingleton to see my girlfriend, and I'm freezing!" I figured the use of the word 'girlfriend', in conjunction with the cold, might help with any doubts with regards giving me a lift, knowing this pleasant teenager, she sort of knew, was prepared to stand in the icy chill, for however long it took, in the name of lust.

"Get in then, we will drop you off." I opened the rear door, thanked Thelma, and began to squeeze into the back. Suddenly the surreal nature of the situation became apparent.

"Come on Cocker, squeeze in," shouted the booming voice of Julie Goodyear, who played the legendary landlady, Bet Lynch. She was safely entrenched in the driver's seat, giant earrings swinging from side to side.

"Here you go duck, plenty of room now," came a voice from the semi-darkness of the back seat where Betty Driver, famous for her fictional hot pots, was seated. I found myself sharing a car journey with three of the most famous actresses of the time, chatting away for the next thirty minutes in a cramped Mini. I will not disclose our conversation as that would be a betrayal of trust (?!) but suffice to say it was a joyous interlude and we all got on very well. I remember telling them that the girl I was visiting called me Penfold. They were incredibly happy to give me their honest advice and support as we hurtled through the country roads. Let's just say I never returned to visit her again.

My girlfriends were always younger and we never seemed to have enough in common. They liked Oasis; I liked The Beatles. They enjoyed tequila slammers; a nice Chardonnay if you please. They appreciated TFI Friday and I relished 'Question Time' on a Thursday. None of them liked dogs either apart from one and that was Susan. She followed my usual preference, so whilst she was playing 'Don't Look Back in Anger' at full throttle, I was engrossed in Eleanor Rigby. She loved a man's best friend though and so it came to pass that we stumbled on renting a house together with my lovely brown retriever, Bonnie, in tow.

Susan was great fun, devoted, had a zest for life but on occasion could be very violent. I never talk about this period of my life. It hurts deeply if I access the memory and, with it, the feelings of humiliation, pain, and denial. It makes me feel extremely uncomfortable but as this book is a journey of the good, the bad and the ridiculous I feel strangely comfortable sharing it with you.

The violence was rare but frightening when it occurred. One extreme example played out at Susan's distant cousin's 50th wedding anniversary. The celebration took place at a remote Country Hotel and was the usual cheesy buffet disco evening some of us are familiar with. A disc jockey mumbling into his microphone with incoherent sentences, the finger buffet that on closer inspection was mostly made up of numerous bowls of chips and, of course, the gin and tonic at £15 a shot.

"I only ordered a single."

"I have only poured you a single, Sir."

"Oh…"

The evening meandered along, and as we all stumbled towards the inevitable last orders, so the arrival of the contemporary classics galvanised our resident DJ with Agadoo, Superman and The Time Warp all taking centre stage, alongside dozens of happy senior citizens.

I am not sure what caused the brutality that ensued. I think it was related to an accusation that I had talked for too long with her female cousin, seventeen times removed. What I do remember is cowering in the corner of our hotel bedroom, curled up by the side of the bed, my hands and arms desperately trying to cover my face as the bedside lamp repeatedly thudded down on me, with a ferocity that was hard to comprehend. I thought being in the foetus position would protect me until I felt the moisture start to run down the side of my cheeks. At first, I imagined it was just frightened sweat from the situation but the realisation that it was blood, and lots of it, soon became apparent.
The aftermath always followed the same pattern and those that have been through it may identify with the following exchange.

"I am so, so sorry… I didn't mean it… I don't know why… I love you so much…"

"It's okay, come on, sit down. You're shaking, it's fine. Everything will be alright. Come and lay here for a while. You will be nice and calm in a minute. I'm just going to pop into the bathroom and clean up a bit."

That was that. Never to be spoken about again. Absolute denial from both of us as to what had just happened. I am sure those in the adjoining rooms must have heard the commotion. As Susan's parents were in one of them, it is likely they were woken, blow by blow.

Breakfast, the next morning, was rather awkward. Eight of us had arranged to meet and share a table, including her parents. So there we were, sat in the beautiful conservatory, the winter sun glistening through the glass panels, with perfectly formed lawns steaming and mixing with the light mist. Not a word was spoken as I delicately ate my bacon and eggs through a half-functioning mouth, with just the one eye available to see what was in front of me. I contemplated asking the waiter for a straw, but this would have required either jaw movement or sign language, neither of which I was able to perform. That breakfast table knew what had happened. No ifs, no buts. It was so obvious. Yet the discussion was all about the disappointing buffet, the prices of the drinks and why their individual song requests had not been actioned. I had this gut wrenching feeling that I was the only one sat around that table who felt any shame, remorse, and humiliation.

So it was that Susan, Bonnie and I moved into our rented semi-detached house, away from our home village. It was closer to the nearest city, offering better career prospects but the estate was very grey and run down. Deep down, I knew that this move was not going to make me happy, firstly due to the toxic nature of the relationship and secondly due to the area we were about to reside in. I convinced myself, as I loaded my life-size print of Marilyn Monroe into the van, that this was what I wanted. A partner to live with and share everything with. A dog and, maybe in time, a discussion with regards the shared joy of children together. You might be thinking, 'Why on earth would he be doing this? This is madness!' Trust me, those who have been in similar situations just do.

At the same time, I had just bagged myself a new sales job and it was here I met Dawn. She was a few years older than me and far more mature. She was given the unenvious role of teaching me the ropes. She did not like me. Not one iota.

She soon made it abundantly clear that it was not to her advantage to teach me anything. She also found my vile, ill-fitting, green suit embarrassing. She wasn't the only one, but it was all I had and gave us some common ground when chatting. I say chatting, more Dawn constantly ribbing me but with just a hint of criticism in every comment. I went along, laughing nervously at her jibes, in the hope that she would grow weary, and instead, start to enjoy my company and not mock my attire.

As the days went by, so Dawn's ambivalent attitude began to thaw, and I liked her. Very much. She was feisty, didn't suffer any fools, and had a sarcastic sense of humour that I adored. She was also a bloody good salesperson, extremely attractive with long auburn hair and huge brown eyes. I found her experience intoxicating and reassuring. Whilst she never did become a fan of David Dimbleby, she drank Chardonnay by the gallon, which was good enough for me.

The days became weeks, and we spent a vast amount of time together in the sales office and then inevitably, the social arena. We would go for a drink after work and then head home in separate directions. These would become more regular and last longer. Was that because I was falling for her and wanted to spend as much time as possible in her company? Or was it because it meant I didn't have to go home, and as such, spend less time with Susan in our sad, tired home. Looking back, I am sure it was a combination of both, but the idea of being with Dawn took an incredible hold on me from an exceedingly early stage.

I had established that Dawn was single. I also knew she had never lived with anyone and liked her own space. That could be a bit of a hurdle to overcome but like most things she told me in our preliminary courtship, I ignored the parts that did not fit with my mental narrative.

We started to have evenings out where she lived. I know what you are thinking. 'How? What about Susan?' The thing is, I did work late so it was easy to have a date with Dawn and not arouse suspicion. I would sometimes get home extremely late but that was the nature of my new job and I was out to impress. Dawn as it transpired, not my employers, who had become a bit of an afterthought.

Dawn was fully aware of Susan from the start. I never hid the fact that I lived with someone, but I certainly did conceal some of the painful elements of that relationship. The dates continued and I vividly remember the first time we kissed. It was in a wine bar in her hometown. A Thursday evening, I recall, relatively quiet, and it just happened. One moment we were laughing about my attire again and the next I had her face gently cupped in my hands as we locked lips for the first time. It was a revelation to me. It is hard to describe but it felt different. How an adult kiss should feel. Mature and comfortable. I won't go into the raunchy details of what happened next but if you are very lucky, I may do a sequel titled Fifty Shades of Dog Hair (?!). In the meantime, with your permission, I will jump a few months into the future when Dawn asked me to pack my things and go and live with her.

Chapter Two:

My initial plan was to tell Susan one evening. Possibly with a locked door between us. This required finding the right moment, to sit her down and confess. I contemplated purchasing some medieval armour in preparation. I also considered telling her in our driveway, with the passenger window down, car running, gear engaged. The problem was that there were a heck of a lot of evenings, never any right times (or so I convinced myself) and so my current world drifted aimlessly for a few weeks. Dawn would ask me every day and I would reassure her that it would be soon, but I could see she was getting frustrated. She probably thought I was having second thoughts, that I didn't want to share my life with her, but then she didn't know the whole truth. In all honesty, I was petrified. Damaged by horrific memories and terrified what this situation could trigger. In the end I didn't tell Susan anything. I just left.

On a rare day off, I just packed a case and walked out. When I say case, it was actually just a rucksack. Some clothes to tide me by, my passport and a toothbrush. I left everything else. All my personal mementoes built up over many years with, and without, Susan. Family photos, music collection, even my beloved Marilyn Monroe. I was partly in the mindset that I was moving many miles away and this was the start of the rest of my life, and as such I wanted nothing to go with me. A clean slate, so to speak, but I was also in a state of panic that she might just walk in unexpectedly, so no risk was taken, and I was gone in under half an hour. I rang Dawn to tell her I was on my way.

On arrival at my new home, Dawn was there to greet me. The subsequent hug was hugely reassuring. I can't explain the relief, and a tear gently trickled down my left cheek as my head rested on her shoulder. I have a feeling she thought it was a tear of joy and I was not about to disprove this or tell her the real reason for my emotional state. When we finally sat down, coffees in hand, the conversation flowed and I outlined what had happened, and that it was simply better this way.

"Right. Let's go and get the rest of your stuff from the car." Dawn jumped up, excited, and headed towards the front door.

I chuckled. "It won't take you long then. I think there is an umbrella and probably a tennis ball in the boot, but that's about all." I lifted my rucksack and placed it on the dining table. "It's all here. My whole life. Ta-da!" I thought it was funny but the expression on Dawn's face was one of bewilderment.

"That's it?! That's ridiculous. Why? Please don't tell me that the only thing in that bag is your bloody green suit?" She was laughing now but very much with astonishment.

"Firstly, the suit has not hitched a ride with me. Secondly, this is a fresh start for me… us… and I think the best thing we can do is get our own stuff together to make this OUR home. You have most of the same music as me, so that's a start. I appreciate I have a slight shortage of clothes, but once I have unpacked this lot…", she was still laughing and shaking her head, "I am heading to Matalan to go crazy and buy a whole new wardrobe. Fifty quid should cover it."

We were both chuckling away, and I felt relaxed for the first time in months. It was Dawn who stopped smiling first, put her hand up to her mouth and lent rather unsteadily against the door frame.

"Oh my god, the tennis ball… Where's Bonnie?" she asked. "What about Bonnie?"

There are, hopefully, not many times in a life when that knot in your stomach materialises. The overwhelming feeling of nausea. When I got the police phone call, with no other family member to hand, informing me that my grandma had died, was one. Or at the age of fourteen, when my High School sweetheart, Gillian, told me I was dumped with the unexpectedly mature words, 'Sometimes you have to be cruel to be kind' was another. The 'Where's Bonnie?' question was the latest, but probably deepest kink yet.

Bonnie wasn't just any dog. She was my first dog. She was a constant partner throughout my mid-adult years. Just the two of us with some infrequent female companionship popping into our lives prior to Susan joining our journey. I had always wanted my own dog. We had the family one when I was growing up and I desperately wanted to replicate that when I had the opportunity. Finally, as time and current job allowed, the chance arrived when I could go and search for that unconditional companion. I wanted a retriever, a dark chocolate one. After a lot of searching, I saw some puppies advertised in a nearby town and I was there like a shot, lying in the middle of a stranger's kitchen floor being nibbled and licked by six of the most gorgeous puppies you will ever see. We managed to get them out in the garden and they were all playing, falling over each other, one or two letting out little high-pitched barks. It was a joyous sight. I say all of them, but I had noticed that there was one detached from all the others, playing on their own, making its own entertainment up, moving a squeaky chicken toy from one area to another and subsequently attempting to bury it. The breeder noticed me staring at this little bundle and gestured for me to go over for a closer look.

"She's a bonny one, isn't she?" he drawled in his deep Yorkshire twang.

"Very much so, Mr. Askew, but I want a dog really."

"Why's that then?" he laughed. "You do know bitches are far more placid and easier to train?"

"Are they?" I replied, surprised. "I didn't know that. I don't know to be honest, I just never thought about having a girl. Showing a bit of male sexism here, aren't I?"

"Each to their own lad, never had any issues with homosexuals, me."

"No, I wasn't saying…"

I cut the sentence short as I didn't feel it was the right setting to have a deep discussion on prejudices and his understanding of them.

I continued to watch this fluffy female and felt myself drawn to her. The independence; being content on her own. She would make the perfect companion.

She then decided to bound up to me, all paws and ears, proudly presenting me with a clump of grass spilling from her tiny jaw.

"Bonny isn't she?" he said for the second time. Yes, she was.

"I will take her please, Mr. Askew," I said, shaking his hand, "and I shall call her Bonnie. Be a tad rude not to now, wouldn't you say?"

And so it was that Bonnie began her brand-new life with yours truly. She loved routine and visits to the pub, where I worked, at closing time. She would explore under the tables, picking up any scraps that had been left from the meals devoured and she was a firm favourite with the locals who were still loitering around as last orders were called. Those early memories are exquisite. We were perfectly suited, although I never did take up burying anything in the garden even if, at certain times, it had crossed my mind once or twice.

I looked at Dawn in horror. She could tell from my face that I had not given her a second thought, that the mention of her name had come as a complete shock to me. I had abandoned her. She was in the house when I left. I even cuddled her a few times as I stuffed the essential garments into my bag, but at no stage did I think about taking her with me. She was probably looking at me, with those dark quizzical eyes, as I shut the front door for the final time.

"You need to go back for her. Now!" Dawn implored, as I sat hunched in a daze.

"I can't D. Not now. Susan will be home and... I need to think." As I did, I suddenly realised that we had never discussed having my furry friend as part of the package. I looked up at Dawn, gentle tears rolling down her cheeks, and suddenly realised she had already made that decision, long ago. I put my head in my hands and silently cried.

Chapter Three:

The next couple of weeks were especially tough. Susan didn't know where I had moved to, but she knew my place of work and bombarded reception with calls and messages. She rang my mobile, in addition to hundreds of texts. I ignored them all. I suppose I was callous enough to believe that she would just give up, move on. Naïve, I grant you, plus I still had the complication of Bonnie and how on earth I could get her back without any contact and so, with much trepidation, I decided to answer her latest call.

I had devised a plan and Operation Dogging was concocted. I know! Not my suggestion! The idea was to gain Susan's trust over several weeks and, once established, ask if I could come over and take Bonnie for a walk. If she agreed, I would go over, take her out and, not return. A dognap I suppose. I had contemplated just stating that I wanted MY dog back and was coming to get her but having not spoken in weeks, plus any chance of Susan harming Bonnie, meant my only option was to go down the devious approach… again.

The first few conversations were hard. Whilst I had been cold-hearted and cowardly, I did feel huge remorse for what I had done and what she would be going through. She called me numerous insulting names. All justified and, mostly, alien to my limited vocabulary. She threatened to come to the office and tell my boss what a total arsehole I was. I'm glad she didn't as my manager would have looked at Susan with a vacant expression, seeing as she was having an affair with Graham from Accounts.

A date was set and so, one Saturday, as Autumn was setting its stall out, I travelled towards my old home and triggered

Operation Dogging. The long journey was consumed with thoughts around what I was going to say. I am not a particularly good liar. Apparently, I have a habit of emphasising the last word of a sentence and letting that word hang longer than is natural, so I had a high sense of vocabulary alert as I arrived. As I walked up the steps to the faded front door, red paint cracking from the weather elements, I took a deep breath and rang the doorbell. The sound of the little-known Oasis song 'Headshrinker' as a chime was not particularly reassuring. Have a peek at the lyrics and you will know what I mean. The door finally opened, and Susan appeared looking dejected but managing a faint smile.

"Hi…You okay?"

Not my best opening line for greeting someone you had spent eighteen months with, and then just buggered off.

"I'm good thanks," she replied, curtly. "You look well. Have you lost weight? Are you eating properly?"

For an instant she made me feel good about myself, until I tried to square the consuming disorder.

"Not sure whether to take that as a compliment or not," I smiled.

"Don't. It's not."

And with that, an uncomfortable silence entered the porch. It felt like hours, just standing there. Susan staring at me with a cold intensity, a look that made me shudder. Thankfully, she broke the unbearable tension.

"Where are you taking her?"

What? Oh shit! I hadn't thought of a place I was never going to.

"Um…Just to the park, let her have a good long play."

I don't think the word 'play' was emphasised too much or that it drifted longer than normal, but I couldn't be sure.

"Which park? We have three. Or have you forgotten already?!" She was looking at me carefully.

"The one with the lake is the biggest and prettiest, so definitely that one," I managed to say calmly.

"Yes, it is. Maybe only the prettiest when we went together though," she smiled sadly.

For a moment, I felt dreadful. A vile horrible man who, having already dismantled her life in such a cruel way, was about to shatter it all over again.

The stilted conversation continued for a while. I didn't get an invite into the house, which was unsurprising, and finally she went in and brought Bonnie, tennis ball lodged in her mouth, to the porch. A dog's most treasured persona is the absolute joy they display when they see their owners when they have been out or away. The unconditional adulation is a wondrous sight to behold.

"Hello Bon, Bon! Come here and give your dad a huge kiss."

Bonnie launched herself at my face as I bent down, and her rasping tongue went into overdrive. It explored every inch of my skin, culminating in washing my ears out with her usual intensity.

"What time will you be back?" Susan asked, as she handed her over to me.

"What time is it now?" I asked, as I slipped back into operation mode. I needed long enough to get home before any suspicions were aroused.

"Just after two."

"Um…Be no later than four. That okay?"

"Yes, that's fine, but no later please as my Mum and Dad are due at four thirty and I don't think they would want to see you here…" Susan's voice trailed off.

"I'm sure they don't, and vice versa to be honest."

"Look after her, won't you? Don't end up losing her in the woods or something daft like that. She's all I've got now…"

Bonnie raced down the steps, pulling me frantically towards my Ford Explorer, eager for the sniff and snoop that was imminent. Susan was looking at me intently from the front door and I wasn't convinced she knew exactly what I was up to. I loaded the excited hound into the boot, the bright green ball embedded in her happy smiling jaw. I gave Susan a wave and faint smile as I got into the car. One final glance and I drove off, through the estate. I made sure I was back on the main road, far away from the scene of the 'crime', before I pulled over into a layby and sent a text to Dawn.

'Operation Dogging a success. Heading back to base. Over and out. xx'

I checked that Bonnie was all settled and looked to pull out and head home. My heart had settled down now and I let out a huge sigh of relief. In the distance I could see blue lights flashing, heading towards me. It looked like an ambulance, so I decided to wait until it had passed. I glanced behind me and Bonnie was already laid down, comfortable on her blanket. I smiled contentedly. As the emergency vehicle came closer, I realised it was a police SUV and was travelling at some speed. It was upon me in no time and suddenly veered into the layby, racing through, and shuddered to a halt right behind me. I didn't know whether to pull out, get out or shout out. I didn't have to wait long as the driver of the police vehicle was by my door, tapping on the window. I wound the window down.

"Hello Sir, is this your vehicle?"

He looked a little startled as he spoke, seeing me for the first time.

"It's a company car…and I think you already know that. Sorry if I have blocked you in…I didn't know you were going to come in here. I was waiting for you to go by."

"We have had a report that this vehicle is stolen, and that the vehicle may also have a dog that belongs to someone else. I can see a dog, so I do have to ask…is it yours?" The officer now looked uncomfortable as he peered at me.

"I will say it again. You know this is a company car, as you have been in the bloody thing many times and you know it's my dog as she has licked you to an inch of your life… in my house… on numerous occasions… while you guzzled cans of MY Boddingtons, Craig."

My older brother stood, still in police stance, staring at me, leaning on the frame of the driver's door, probably mulling over how on earth he was going to handle this rather embarrassing situation.

"Don't call me Craig, please. This is an official callout, so I just need to deal with it. Stay calm, answer my questions and hopefully you can be on your way."

Stay calm? Hopefully be on your way? What is he going on about?

I can just see it now. He arrests me, I get charged with dognapping, I plead not guilty and call him as my star witness where he will admit to my defence counsel and the jury how well he knew both the defendant and dog in question...

"Okay, ask away, but it's all a bit daft, isn't it?"

I decided to get out of the car and we both leant on the side of the vehicle as I continued to shake my head as the procedure kicked in.

"Can you confirm that you visited 39 Harley Close this afternoon, at approximately one thirty?"

"Yes."

"Did you take the dog that I can see in the back from that address?"

"Yes."

"Did you state you were taking the dog for a walk but returning her?"

"Yes."

"So, you admit taking her?"

"Yes."

"Are you taking her back?"

"No."

"Why not?"

"Because Craig...sorry...Officer... she is MY dog, and she is going to MY new home. The one that YOU are visiting next weekend with your wife Lisa."

Craig continued, serious face unmoved, "You could argue that what you have done is classed as deception, don't you think? As well as stealing a dog?"

"I suppose so. Although as she is mine, you could flip it the other way and query whether Susan was holding Bonnie hostage, like Terry Waite, but your call Officer..."

"Can you prove the dog in the car belongs to you, Sir?" Craig asked, ploughing on.

"Yes, I can...I will just ask you to confirm..." and with that last sentence Craig realised that the situation, that was rather uncomfortable, needed to conclude.

"Okay, I think I will take this back as a domestic dispute and leave you two to sort it out. Not one for me to get involved in." He closed his little pocketbook. "You can be on your way now, Sir."

"Thanks, Officer. Sorry if you have been inconvenienced."

I got back in my car; told a rather excitable Bonnie, who had now spotted Uncle Craig, to lie down, and prepared to depart.

"See you next Saturday then," I said, out of the window.

"Yes, see you then. We should be with you about mid-day. Do we need to bring anything?"

"No, just yourselves," and with that he slowly marched back to his blues and twos, as I set off for the long journey home.

Chapter Four:

As I drove through the countryside, and back to my new life with Dawn, I began to contemplate who I was, what I was, and where I was going. I had just turned thirty and as I meandered towards the motorway, I realised that this was the final goodbye to my youth. A farewell to long-standing friends, and a bye-bye to the beautiful, but stifling, Yorkshire Dales.

You might be thinking how sad I must have felt, but believe me, I was relieved, ecstatic even, as the nature of village life had taken its toll. I had grown out of love with my surroundings many years ago. The endless repetition of living in an area with literally nothing to do. Our nearest cinema was sixteen miles away and even that had just one screen. Damp burgundy seats with protruding springs that gave you piles, and the 80s mega hit Top Gun with top billing. In 1996.

Our weekend routines, looking back, were just so bloody monotonous. We had five pubs. On a Friday and Saturday evening we would visit them in the same order. We left each one at the same time. I cannot remember EVER saying, "Actually lads, I think I am going to stay here and have another." Nobody would have known what to do. How to handle that curve ball. We were like alcoholic robots, pre-programmed from our respective homes. It would have been a slight improvement if there had been a couple of alternative applications we could have pressed, but we only had the one setting.

The only time I escaped this madness was when I actually worked, for a couple of years, in one of the 'Famous Five'. I enjoyed the wet trade very much and our establishment had the cleanest pumps, and best beer in the area, whilst I was in charge. I would like to say it was pride that motivated me, but the truth is, that once I realised that you had to sample the different brews after the cleaning process, I found myself pumping chemicals on a Monday, Wednesday, and Friday at 9.30 am sharp.

As I entered my roaring twenties, so my friends started to settle down, marry and have children. It wasn't quite compulsory, but in reality, with sod all to do, marriage, and the planning of, was a welcome distraction to the endless Groundhog Day of living in such a barren existence. Having children was the same. Another distraction for a while, but the truth was that most of these couplings were built on nothing more than boredom. Between my twentieth birthday and that moment I was driving home to Dawn, the majority had got hitched, had a couple of kids, and were now divorced. All incredibly sad.

I never fell into that trap. I am not sure if it was a subconscious thing that, one day, I was determined to leave this all behind and prosper in a big city. My frequent trips to London to see Louise had whetted my appetite for the excitement of a vibrant life with restaurants and theatres. It was intoxicating and I wanted to be part of it. I did like Louise, very much, but I was far too young to contemplate a big move and fairly sure she wouldn't have welcomed it either. There was a short period, in our relationship, that things might have worked out differently, and that was the day she told me she was pregnant.

We were sat in her halls of residence flat. She had requested an urgent visit, so there I was lying on her bed as she broke the news. How should an eighteen-year-old male respond? If this had been back in village life we would have shrugged, planned, and executed a marriage forthwith. We would then go on to live, not very happily after, with our baby Beardsley.

Let's be brutally honest here. I was incredibly young. I lived in a village. My teenage perspective was based on pubs, sport and the sort of pranks that involved hiding huge ham joints, overflowing with jelly, in a mate's bed. Like a cheap scene out of The Godfather. I had never, at this point, contemplated being a father, or behaving responsibly, and I was acutely aware I was nowhere near ready.

Louise was quite clinical with her announcement, which was not entirely surprising, given her nursing occupation, but she was also quite cold and matter of fact. An announcement devoid of any emotion, so any chance that my instinct and brain would react in a euphoric manner were butchered before she had finished.

"What should we do?" she asked, but in a way that wasn't really a question.

"It's entirely up to you, Lou. It has to be your decision," I said with respect. "I will support you in whatever you decide is for the best."

A ridiculous statement in hindsight. I didn't even support her right there and then. Just passed the buck. For all I know, she wanted me to hug her tight, tell her it was going to be alright, that we should embrace this little life that would come into our world. That whatever happened in the future, I would always be there for them both. But I didn't.

"It will never work. It would never work. I have my career," she said sadly. "Thanks for your honesty."

The last sentence confused me, but I never challenged it. The shameful truth is that I wanted to be out of that room right then. Even worse, out of her life forever. I couldn't handle it. At that moment I would have given anything to be back in my narrow, sheltered life in the Dales.

We made small talk for a while. I offered, with no real conviction, that we should go out for dinner, but the reality was that we were just stalling until I could catch my super-saver late train home.

As the train rattled through the darkness, my thoughts turned to what was going to happen in the near future. I should have felt guilt, a huge sense of loss; but I felt neither. I had a duty to support Louise with what she was about to go through; her loss and pain, but I blocked that emotion out too. I was just relieved to be going back to a normal life with no complications and no responsibilities. What kind of man can act like that? A very scared eighteen-year-old, that's who.

How life could have turned out differently, I thought, as I got closer to Dawn, leaving the last of the motorways for the final short segment to home. I was sure that I would not still be with Louise, but I would have a twelve-year-old son or daughter who I would have loved with all my heart. The majority of the time, I made a conscious effort not to think about what might have been but sometimes, when I did, it became all consuming. A tsunami of regret that was hard to shake off. It didn't help that Peter Beardsley was in his prime for many of the subsequent years, parading his talents on Match of the Day, so it was all too easy to be bounced straight back into the past, as his face filled the TV screen after another of his mesmerising goals.

I would picture a beautiful imaginary face. Sometimes a girl, other times a boy, but so clear and real. My invention would run riot, from holding Louise's hand as she gave birth, to long visits to London and vice versa to the Yorkshire Dales. A child who grew up with the hustle and bustle of city life, but an appreciation of the beauty and laid-back nature of a nosey village. An appreciation of two quite different types of life, without being trapped. Would they be musical? Or sporty? I had decided they would be intelligent; so taking after their mother I supposed.

I never spoke with Louise again or kept in touch via other means. We never came to that decision, clinically, but there was an unsaid, mutual acceptance that it was over and that she would get on with her life and career and I would do the same, although the latter was significantly lacking for yours truly. First Louise and now Susan. Both deserted without an explanation, no empathy or respect. Some of you might forgive me for the latter toxic, abusive relationship and I would probably concur. Not Lou though. Please don't forgive me for this one, or our unborn child, as I will never forgive myself.

As I finally pulled up outside the house, with Bonnie staring out of the window with her tongue flapping from side to side, I knew this was it. This was adult time. Set the dial to grown-up position. It had its risks, and the greatest was the probability that I would never have children now. At forty-two, Dawn was unlikely to desire them and even if she did, the pressure, stress, and time against us, could prove insurmountable.

I was okay with this. I think. I hope. I got out of the car and made a pact to myself. Love Dawn, love life, and don't ever watch Match of the Day again.

Chapter Five:

Dawn, Bonnie, and I soon settled into our new life together. I had a few more weeks of missed calls and text messages from Susan, but they got less frequent as the days went by, and finally came to an end. That chapter of my life was now closed for good and buried deep in my memory. Dawn and I carried on working at the same company and would travel separately to work each day and then race one another home on the motorway. A bit immature, and not particularly law-abiding, but we enjoyed seeing who could get home first. Who could find a new back road to gain an advantage? Dawn was usually the victor, but then she was born and bred in the area so had an edge in planning and plotting different routes. This childish behaviour came to an end when I secured a new sales role close to home and, by default, I was the winner from that day on.

Our lives were as average as most couples and we were happy in each other's company. We walked Bonnie of course, enjoyed cooking together, shared copious amounts of white wine and as she had seven siblings (!), plus their children, we spent most weekends in the company of one, some, or all of them. It was through her interaction with her nephews and nieces that I began to see Dawn's love of children. Whilst it brought me joy, at times I felt a deep pang of sadness with my past. She was a perfect auntie. Always playing with them and thinking up new and unique games to entertain. She was kind, thoughtful, loving and I could tell she adored being around them. Since moving in together, we had never discussed the idea of having children, but I had already come to my mental conclusion. In conversations with her friends, it was obvious she felt that the opportunity had passed her by, and that age was against her. I understood that and it didn't change how I felt or that we wouldn't be together. Some things are more important and being a couple was enough for me. I was determined that would always be the case.

I soon settled into my new job and enjoyed being closer to home. I missed being with Dawn through the day, but it had many advantages and was far healthier in the long term if our relationship was to thrive and develop. We kept in touch sporadically by text and shared our work stories every evening, rather than discussing what we both already knew from being in the same building.

I had just left an internal meeting about a meeting we had last week, in preparation for a meeting we were having next week (!) when my Blackberry rang. It was Dawn. This was rare, as our interaction through a working day usually consisted of flirty or funny messages.

"Hiya D, everything okay?" I spoke as I strode through the corridor, heading for the next tedious meeting.

"Yeh, I'm fine. Can you get home a bit earlier tonight? I have a half-day off now so will be home soon, and I have something to show and share with you." She sounded a bit flustered, possibly a bit excited, but I wasn't sure on the bad line.

"Of course I can. Any clues though? Is it a present?"

"Just get your arse back here and you will find out. Text me when you are on your way."

With that, she ended the call. I was intrigued. The rest of the day seem to drag on endlessly, but I managed to sneak away an hour early and I let Dawn know that I was on my way.

The hallway was dimly lit as I hung my coat up. Bonnie rushed up for her usual fuss and I poked my head into the living room. The log fire was flickering but otherwise empty of life. A quick wander into the dining room, followed by the kitchen, showed no sign of Dawn either. I called her name with just a tinge of panic.

"D?"

"Up here, in the bedroom."

I climbed the stairs, stopping momentarily to let Bonnie bundle past me, and entered our bedroom. Dawn was sat on the rocking chair in the corner of the room swinging gently back and forth.

"Come on then, what's the big surprise? Show and share you said. Time to show!"

Dawn lifted her hand up and waved a small thin object in my direction. I hadn't the faintest idea what it was, partly because she was still rocking like Norman Bates's mother, so it was hard to focus. I moved closer and could see the item more clearly now. It was blue and white and looked like a cross between a thermometer and a sort of magic marker highlight pen. Still no idea.

"What is it? You have me D. I have no idea what you are trying to show me, let alone share."

"You are joking, right? You are having me on?" She was shaking her head.

"No!" I exclaimed. "Why would I be joking? What is it?"

"Here, take it. Have a good look and you tell me. I can wait." She placed it in my hand and I just stared at it, turning it over in my hands, still not knowing what on earth I was looking at, but with a growing realisation that it was some sort of thermostat, possibly a test of some sort. Yes, a test…a type of test…A TEST…and suddenly it hit me like a Nigel Benn uppercut. My facial expression must have been one of disbelief.

"Ah…I think you have a good idea now." Dawn was still rocking in the chair. "I cannot believe you didn't know. I thought you were trying to wind me up, build some sort of suspense."

"Honestly, D, I had absolutely no idea…I don't know what to say…" The excitement inside was bursting to get out and I could feel myself shaking.

You are probably reading this and rolling your eyes with disbelief. Of course he must have known it was a pregnancy test. Everyone knows what one of those is!

I didn't. Why would I? I had never been lucky enough to be in that situation before. Louise had informed me after she had confirmation, and I had certainly not wandered around Boots trying to find the pregnancy test aisle. Whilst some TV programmes may have given me a hint, I didn't watch oodles of drama and I am fairly sure Question Time never covered them in its long and distinguished history. It had never crossed my mind that this was the reason Dawn wanted me home early. We were responsible adults, and that meant we were taking the usual precautions. Dawn brought me round from my dazed expression.

"Shall I go and do it then?"

"Do it? You mean you haven't done it yet?" Now I was confused, my brain scrambled.

"No. I wanted you to be here. So that we can share it. Find out together. Back in a mo."

Dawn headed to the bathroom and I had a few seconds to catch my thoughts. Is this it? Is this the moment when the twelve years of pain are vanquished. An image of Louise popped into my head. Then a picture of an imaginary child. A teenager. I shook my head to clear my mind. Now is what matters, damn it, NOW.

We sat on the bed. The streetlight was gently flickering through the curtains. We held hands tightly as we stared at the test intensely.

The next few minutes were a bit of a blur to be honest. I remember the magic marker hitting the wardrobe with such force that it shattered into pieces. I recall some of the words she shouted. 'NO' was the first, second and third, followed by a flurry of swear words that would require googling later. I looked at the fragments on the carpet and the image of the teenager returned with a vengeance.

Chapter Six:

Dawn was still on the bed. She was curled up, knees under her chin and was sobbing uncontrollably. I was now on the floor, gathering the bits from the carpet. Not because I was still trying to get confirmation of the result. The two positive lines were conclusive. I was just finding something to do whilst I gathered my thoughts.

I was sobbing too. But this was confined to my inner self. Whilst my hidden tears were of happiness and surprise, there was no doubt that the opposite was true from my inconsolable partner who was sitting a few feet away.

It was undeniable that I had misread the situation. My own selfish thoughts and dreams had completely disregarded what Dawn was pondering as we had waited for the result.

I stayed on the floor for far longer than was necessary. I was unable to decipher what to do next, how to handle this highly charged emotional situation. What do I say? What can I say?

I think I would have stayed down there forever if Dawn hadn't broken the uncomfortable silence.

"I can't…I can't do this…I don't want this. I'm sorry." She was sat up, the tears seemingly drained from her, eyes red raw. The sadness in her face was agonising to witness and I dragged my weary, deflated body up from the floor and joined her on the bed.

"Come here. It's okay. I love you so very much. That's all that matters."

We embraced and held each other so tightly that I could feel her heart pounding against my chest and the tears flowed again, this time from us both. It was like déjà vu for me, with the difference of reaction down to both previous experience and maturity. That is not to say I was conflicted in my response. Should I tell her? Would it help? Do I really want this child to right a wrong from many years ago?

I stirred the milk into the mugs as I stared out of the kitchen window. It was dark but the lit lanterns swayed in the breeze, in the back garden, as I watched the next-door neighbour's cat toying with a mouse; the poor thing about to meet its fate but only when the feline had got bored with the entertainment.

Dawn had gone to the bathroom whilst I made us a cup of tea. I had suggested something stronger, but this was declined. I felt a sense of unity was required so, however much I craved the largest glass of vino I could get my hands on, Yorkshire Tea it was.

I was still in a daze with the situation and whilst deep down I was desperate to convince her that we should be parents, that we would make great parents, I was acutely aware that whatever happened from this point onwards I would need to respect and support her final decision. Our lives were not going to be determined by us having children. It wasn't in our plans a few hours ago and I needed to concentrate on that mindset. An unexpected birth will either happen and be embraced by us both; or it won't, and our expected path of life will continue to wherever the stars align and take us in the future. All of that statement was true, but I knew the reality could be quite different, especially for my mindset.

Lying back on the bed, side-on, we faced each other and finally talked. We opened up to each other with searing honesty. We communicated as never before and, in hindsight, should have done right at the beginning when we made the rash, but thrilling, decision to throw caution to the wind and live together. It took a while to get to that point though.

"Tell me what you are thinking?" I asked, as I gently stroked her long auburn hair. "Be totally honest."

"What are you thinking?" she replied.

"Doesn't matter what I am thinking, it's you that matters. So tell me."

"It does matter. I need to know what you're thinking."

"Honestly? It's not important at the moment. Far more important to know how you feel. What your thoughts are," I said, slightly exasperated.

"You first. Promise I will say how I feel after you have."

"No chance!" I replied, my voice getting louder. "Just start. Say something and I promise it will just flow. I will just listen."

"Please. I need to hear what you have to say," Dawn implored.

On we went, back and forth, neither being the first to say how we felt deep down. Ridiculous behaviour. Both frightened of saying the wrong thing in this delicate situation.

We both had the faintest of smiles, the first for a while, as I decided to take the plunge and tell her my truth. Well, some of it. If we were going to get through whatever decision we made, she had to know my feelings right now. At this moment. She didn't need to know the past.

"Okay," I began, "Twenty minutes ago was the best moment of my life. When I saw those little lines appear, however briefly, I can't describe the elation I felt. I know we have never talked about it... about children... what a fantastic mum you would be... and to be honest I had given up hope of having any."

"Hope?" Her voice suddenly high pitched.

"Hope is the wrong word. Sorry. I mean I had just resigned myself to not having any. It would have happened years ago if it were meant to be. Then I met you, fell in love and so that was that."

"That was that? What was that?" She was getting rather animated.

"That I wouldn't have children, but that was okay as we had each other, and this was my life and I was fine with it. I think."

"You think? Why wouldn't you have children with ME? Why did you think that?" She was gently smiling, but there was a slight steel to her gaze.

"Because you didn't want them, and I was okay with that. Also, I know you felt...I don't know...that maybe time had passed you by. That if we had met earlier...you know what I mean..."

"I don't. I really don't! How on earth do you know that I don't want children? Are you insinuating that I am too bloody old...at forty-two...?" Dawn let out a shriek.

"Don't blame me," I interrupted. "Your friends made it clear you were never the broody type and I know you are not too old...I just thought YOU thought you were."

I threw my hands in the air.

"Oh, for god's sake!" I yelled. "You don't think you are do you?"

I started to laugh, and I pulled her in close and gave her a gentle kiss.

"If you hadn't just said what you did," Dawn explained, "about being elated and it being the best moment of your life, then we wouldn't be carrying on this conversation."

Dawn laid her head on my lap, looking up to the ceiling, as she continued, "I hardly know you... not that well anyway. Six months we have been together, that's all. How can we have a child? What if this doesn't work out? What happens as I get older? What about complications? My age? I have never had to think about any of those things. Bloody good reason for that too. Being on my own and not having to contemplate emotional shit like this."

She tailed off on the last sentence, but I could gauge that she wanted to say more so I stayed silent.

"I don't know if you want to stick around," she continued. "I have... had... no idea you want or wanted a child with me. Or if you have ever wanted children with anyone. We have never talked about it. Think about the change in our lives... my life. I have been on my own for so long and then you come along and just as I am beginning to get used to you... us... I have to consider someone else coming along. I can't... it's too much, too soon. It won't work. It will spoil it all. My age doesn't help either..."

This was the second time she had brought up her age and for the first time I felt I knew. Of course, she wanted a baby. It was probably a burning desire, like mine, which circumstances had dampened as the years went by. We had both assumed, wrongly, that we were too late.

"I was right about the age thing then, wasn't I?" I said, playfully. "Come on admit it. Let me have one little victory in all this."

I squeezed her arm, as she slapped my chest and smiled.

"You scared?" I whispered.

"Too right, I'm bloody scared. You?"

"Absolutely petrified... but if deep down you want this baby... OUR baby, then forget about this ridiculous age argument, as it means nothing. I want to be with you whatever you decide but, yes, I want us to have this child together. I promise you I will be with you every frightening and thrilling second of the journey to come. It has to be your decision though, but I love you very much and I promise to support you, whatever you decide."

I lifted my head skywards and let out a silent sigh as I waited. There was a long pause.

"You will have to pull your finger out then and get the spare room cleaned out," she said, as she buried her head, deep into my chest.

The ceiling was the first lucky recipient to see my ecstatic reaction.

"I will start at the weekend," I stated with a false nonchalance. "Although you are fit enough to give me a hand for a while yet, you know."

We looked at each other. A combination of smiles, fear, and excitement engulfing our faces.

Dawn nodded off in my arms, so I gently eased away and gathered myself in the bathroom. I sat on the toilet seat, staring at our Kermit and Miss Piggy dressing gowns hanging from the door. A mixture of emotions oozed from every pore, as a dashboard of memories exploded through my brain. Bet Lynch, Louise, Susan, that hotel breakfast table, my adorable Bonnie and then finally, for the last time, the familiar reoccurring image of a child, who would have been twelve, smiling at me. I am not religious, at all, but I leant forward, put my head in my hands and whispered to myself.

"To whoever might be watching over me. Thank you."

Chapter Seven:

I cannot describe the change in my personality once the reality of becoming a father started to sink in. Overnight I became, how should I put it? Soft! Well, softer in all honesty, as I was a very laid-back, genial type anyway, but suddenly I was even more understanding and tolerant of everything around me.

I detest queuing but I suddenly found that I didn't mind being at the back of Morrisons with what looked like thirty-five trolleys in front of me. To be fair, this was on Christmas Eve, when families seemed to have grown invisible children and long-lost cousins to feed, but in the past I would have been raging inside, sneakily blocking people from aisles or 'accidentally' knocking a bottle of Crofts Original from the summit of their grotesque mountain of Twiglets.

Now I was quite happy just to wait my turn, moving closer to the young student on till four every ten minutes or so, daydreaming of what was to come and how my life, suddenly, felt fulfilled. I have to say though that my softer side was put to the ultimate test when my credit card failed and the customers behind me, unaware of my newfound peace, were not in the same place mentally.

"We need to prepare and prepare properly!"

These were the words Dawn expressed on the morning after our wonderful, unexpected news but I had no idea what she meant until her details, a few weeks later, were forthcoming. I knew we would be making lists of what we would need, that the spare room would need sprucing up, etc., but some of the planning she had in mind hadn't crossed *my* mind.

"Right. Preparation is not always about material things, okay?"

She was laying on the sofa, Bonnie curled up by her feet. I had ended up on the floor for some reason, with my head resting on the battered arm. Dawn looked different. It was hard to explain but she just looked lovelier than ever, with a contented demeanour.

"I think so ... What things were you thinking? Whatever you need."

"I'm glad you said that as from now I need to stop drinking and I think it would be helpful if you supported me and did the same."

It was a good job she couldn't see my expression. The reality that my bucket-load of Chardonnay had just vanished was etched in a frown that I feared would become permanent. How I cursed being so encouraging! Shamefully my thoughts, instead of reacting with complete support, were frantically thinking of all the places I could hide a bottle and the times of the day or evening I would be on my own and could take a sneaky slurp. Contemptible I know but I couldn't help my brain trail at that precise moment.

"Of course I will. We are in this together," I said, as a spot behind the old piano in the garden shed became my imaginary storing place for the bottles that still needed some love and attention from time to time.

I never did taste a drop. Once the shock of not having something that had become the norm for the past decade had subsided, it was extremely easy to support Dawn. If I ever felt badly done to or felt sorry for myself when certain requests came my way, I would just think back to the day before 'magic marker' night and the reminder, at that exact point in my life I was going to be a father. How can anything be a burden when you put those two feelings side by side?

One of the main tasks entrusted to me was to research and purchase a pram. You would think this would be easy but it was like choosing a new car. So much choice. Different weights, suspension, wheels, etc. Buggies that can take on all terrains or are just for smooth transportation. Some were so luxurious that I am sure you could have requested air conditioning if so desired.

It was all a bit confusing for me, so I was relieved when my mum said she had one in the loft at home, and it was ours if we wanted it. Having looked at the cost of a Mamas & Papas top-of-the-range pram, with alligator leather as standard, I accepted her kind offer and imagined how happy Dawn would be with my ingenuity.

On the pretence of 'I should really go and see Mum', I made the long trip back to the Yorkshire Dales to collect our baby Bentley. I had a love-hate relationship with the journey to my childhood home. The hate came from the distance, some painful memories, and the endless single-lane roads, but the love came from the extraordinary countryside and views. They were always breathtaking and outweighed the slow meandering progress, although this particular trip became one of my saddest trips as it coincided with the Foot and Mouth outbreak that devastated the agriculture industry in 2001. I vividly remember the giant lorries and trailers in laybys, watching the conveyer belts in motion. The carcasses of cows, one by one, slowly rising up the machines and being dropped unceremoniously into the trailers. You could hear each thud from the comfort of your own car. It was heart-breaking and the slow trickle of tears were persistent throughout the fifteen miles of devastation.

I rarely visited my mum. This was mostly down to the aforementioned journey but it was also because both our lives had moved on in such different directions. After my father scuttled away, when I was thirteen, we had to pack up and leave our four-bedroomed converted barn and find something a tad smaller. And cheaper. I moved out of our 'family' cramped one-bedroomed bedsit as soon as the clock pinged on my sixteenth birthday. I left school, got a job, a flat, and made best friends with the likes of Thelma, Julie and Betty. I needed space. When you have spent the best part of three years sharing a bedroom with your older brother, a younger sister who slept in the boiler cupboard with her feet sticking out of the door frame like the wicked witch of the north, and a mum who had to bed down in the living room, you cannot wait to have the space to do cartwheels in your own environment.

Mum then met a lovely 'blunt as they come' Yorkshireman and I bagged myself a stepdad at the grand old age of eighteen. Mum and I always remained close, just not the tight us-against-the-world bond that had consumed us all in those early years.

I never looked in the box. After a pleasant cup of tea, I heaved the carton down from the loft and into the boot. A kiss on both cheeks, the Spanish way, and I was on my way back, feeling giddy at the surprise that Dawn was about to receive and the brownie points coming my way.

I laid out the box, still sealed, in our living room and waited for her to arrive back from work. Bonnie seemed to be overly excited by the contents and spent a long time circling, sniffing, and licking the outside. It had been up in a loft for a while so there were many different smells for her to enjoy.

On her return, I ushered Dawn into the lounge, my hands over her eyes. The 'Ta-da' as I removed them, so she could see what was in front of her, was immensely satisfying.

"What is it?"

"Open it!" I implored excitedly.

Dawn gently pulled the flaps away and stared at the contents.

"What the hell is that?!" she screamed and I moved alongside and peered in.

What the hell indeed. First the good news. It was definitely a pram. It had wheels. It had bars. The bad news was that it looked like something out of the 1960s. Actually, scrub that, it *was* from the 60s. 1963 at a guess. The year my brother Craig was born. Don't ask me why it had not crossed my mind. My defence was that I was a father-to-be and, as such, my head was all mushy and gooey.

"My baby is not going to be carried around in that! I will look like I am in a bloody black and white documentary!"

"*Our* baby…" I pointed out.

"Yes okay. Our baby. Even bloody worse. Do you want to be seen walking past the neighbours with this? Christ, the wheels are thinner than our pizza cutter."

"I get your point but…"

It was no good, she was away and, in this mood, she took some stopping.

"Just take it back. I will find one. It really is not hard. We just need a simple, hard-wearing thing that can be bashed about, pack up neatly and last until he or she can ruddy walk."

I gently whispered, "Ah…well… it's a gift actually, so nowhere to take it back."

"Is this why you went to your mother's?"

I could see the little dimples in her cheek getting larger as her mouth got wider.

"I get it now. Did it not cross your mind that it might have been from the Victorian age? It's probably not even safe now. It won't even have a kite thingy."

The Victorian jibe was slightly harsh but she had a valid point. Not sure what she meant about the kite though, as I hadn't seen any on the market with this recreational option.

"You're right D. I'm sorry. I never gave it a thought. I just thought of the saving… Anyway, leave it with me. I will put it together, clean it up and whack it on eBay. Should get a few quid, and mum doesn't really need to know. If she visits I will tell her it's gone for an annual service…"

Dawn smiled and, as had become the norm lately, put her hands onto her ever-growing bump and rubbed away gently.

I am no DIY expert. In fact, I renamed it G.AN.E many years ago. Get an expert. Having said that, I felt obliged to put this ramshackle pram together and make it look enticing for any rather odd people looking for this type of thing. I was immensely proud of myself when it stood there, all shiny and magnificent. It was also quite sentimental to know that this was how I had probably travelled around when I was a young bairn.

I was, and am still, not a frequent eBay user but whenever I have used it, I have been strangely drawn by the countdown as the bids increase in the last few minutes. Mind you, the last time I had any dealings was with a few rolls of zebra wallpaper (don't ask!) that had a reserve price of £1. The deflation, seeing the countdown only reach £1.25 as the auction came to an end, burst the bubble for a while.

I decided to list for just a week only and get rid of the darn thing. 'One Silver Cross Balmoral pram for sale. Colour navy. Circa 1963. Good condition. Collection only.'

I didn't put a reserve on it and waited to see if anyone would bother to even look at it, let alone bid on the darn thing. By the time the last hour of the auction had come round, I had a bid of £75 (wow!) but a good number 'watching'. I settled down to see if the price could squeeze a little higher by the time going, going, gone came.

Then it started. I just sat mesmerised as the price went up and up. Changing every few seconds as the bidders kept chipping in a bit more. By the time the imaginary gavel had come down, Fiona Ryedale, from Richmond in Yorkshire, had become the proud new owner at the … wait for it … extortionate amount of £1,148.

I stood up in a daze, ambled into the kitchen and gathered my thoughts. No need to bother my mum with the news was my first thought. My second thought was the realisation that our baby could now have the best pushchair ever, with alligator leather, if I so desired.

I sat at the kitchen table, with a contented smile across my face, and poured myself an exceptionally large glass of chilled, non-alcoholic wine.

Chapter Eight:

The weeks flew by and, before we had both caught our breath, we were just a month away from the scheduled birth. We were incredibly lucky. It was uncomplicated and Dawn rarely suffered any issues. The bump got bigger, she looked lovelier and our excitement built, day by day, towards this whole new chapter in our lives.

We never signed up for any clinics or baby classes so the only interactions with any professionals were the two ultrasound appointments that were required. The first was one of the most surreal, emotional experiences of my life. Sat on a chair, holding Dawn's hand, as the camera searched and found this tiny silhouette was humbling in so many ways. Tears were rolling down Dawn's cheeks, her smile as wide as Wallace and Gromit, as she gripped my fingers. I was in awe at what I was watching in front of me. My eyes became rather blurred through the optic waterfall that was forming and I had an overwhelming desire to protect both of them. The picture, given to us as we left, is still in my wallet; a bit worse for wear I grant you, but with me nonetheless.

It was at the second scan that our naivety was fully exposed. We knew our baby would be checked for height and weight, that the organs would be inspected, but when the nurse asked us if we would like to know the sex we were flummoxed.

We had, of course, talked about whether we would be having a boy or girl but we had forgotten that we could find out before they said 'Hello' to the world. So there we were, in a noticeably quiet room, debating heatedly on the pros and cons of knowing if we were going to have Terry or June.

I was all for it. Preparation was important and it would give me a steer on pink or blood red for the bedroom, but Dawn was all for the surprise element as the birth unfolded.

"The trouble is," I stated in a bombastic manner, "when I was born, I was called George for a month just for popping out on St George's Day. They had no idea what to call me and took a bloody age to decide, which was rather confusing for family and friends when they finally made a decision and I was called someone completely different."

"That has nothing to do with it," she retorted. "They could have made a list of both, then chosen one of each. Job done. It's not hard."

She had a valid point and I made a mental note to ask my mother why on earth she hadn't a clue what to call me when I came along.

"It's up to you, D. I can live with either scenario," I said, genuinely.

Dawn looked at the nurse. She was smiling at us but I did detect a 'what a couple of idiots' look in her eyes but I would never be able to prove it.

"We don't want to know, thank you."

She then angled her head towards me.

"We shall make a list of both and choose one."

Job done indeed.

I happen to believe that this decision fundamentally changed me. Not in any deep or meaningful way but, to this day, I can leave presents unopened. They can be left on a table for days, sometimes weeks, and I will keep looking at them and get a tingle of excitement over and over again. I think I want to relive the whole 'boy or girl' feeling and this, in a ridiculously small way, gives me the same buzz.

We gave ourselves a month to come up with separate names and then reconvene. Those we had both written down would go on the shortlist. One evening, after dinner, we settled down to share lists and decide. I drew the short straw and read out my 'register'. Girls' names first.

"Right," I started confidently, rolling out my A4 sheet like a certificate. "I have Kristin, Demi, Whitney, Catherine, Olivia, Diana and Michelle."

"That's an interesting and diverse list," Dawn replied, in a quizzical and slightly sarcastic manner. "What made you like those in particular?"

"I just think they are lovely, and a good mixture. Both traditional and modern," I said proudly.

"So, nothing to do with you fancying them all then?"

"What?" I screamed. "That's ridiculous. What do you mean, fancy? They are just names I like. You can be so shallow sometimes."

I was genuinely hurt. I did just like them. I think.

"Okay, I'm sorry. I just thought. Do you mind if I test out my theory?"

"Go for your life. Happy to prove you wrong."

"Kristin? Is that the Kristin Scott Thomas you fancied in Four Weddings and a Funeral?"

I shuffled uncomfortably.

"Well, I hadn't thought of it that way."

"Demi? Moore by any chance?" she exclaimed with conviction.

"Possibly. Okay, maybe those two have scrambled my emotional brain, but the others ..."

Dawn was now sitting up, her wondrous bump just inches away from me.

"Oh, this is going to be good. Whitney? Let me see. Whitney Houston, from that film The Bodyguard. The one I catch you watching from time to time?"

"Alright. I will give you that one."

"Catherine? As in Bach from The Dukes of Hazzard?"

This was getting embarrassing.

"Could be any bloody Catherine, but now you mention it," I said, deflated.

"Olivia? Let me guess. The one from Grease?"

She was enjoying this far too much.

"Diana? Has to be the people's Princess? So bloody obvious. You are always banging on about her, and how much you miss her. I think that just leaves Michelle?"

"Ah, you see!" I said triumphantly. "Not all of them are desired in my imagination."

"Not much of a defence is it?" she laughed. "Just one out of six? Anyway, I haven't finished yet."

She pretended to contemplate.

"Michelle had me perplexed for a moment but then I remembered that we watched Dangerous Liaisons together and you proudly stated she was gorgeous. So my educated guess is Michelle Pfeiffer. Am I right?"

As a game, Dawn was loving it and bloody hell she was good at it. For me, it was damning and shallow. I had legitimately written them down with a liking for each one. It was the subconscious me that was my undoing.

"I am so shallow," I exclaimed sadly.

"Don't be daft." She leant over and stroked my cheek. "My list has George, Rob, Don, and Mickey. Want to try and get your own back?"

We were now laughing; so loudly that poor Bonnie was startled from her deep sleep.

"Let's see," I said, rubbing my chin with fake intelligence. "This might be easier than I first thought. Okay, I am going to go for Clooney, Lowe, Johnson and Rourke."

"Spot on." She was triumphant in her reaction. "Say hello to Mr and Mrs Superficial."

"Christ, have we any names on the lists that we don't want to sleep with?" I asked despondently.

"Well, I have Charlotte on my list," Dawn replied in a loving tone.

"I have Daniel on mine. Any Daniels you would like to share a bed with?" I asked with a glint in my eye.

"Not that I can think of," she mused. "Any Charlottes you lust over?"

"Nope. None that I can think of. I like Charlotte. It's a beautiful name."

"So is Daniel. Let's get rid of the lists, shall we?"

She collected them both, tore them slowly into small pieces and threw them on the table like confetti. A huge smile of satisfaction etched on her face as she sat back down and, with her now familiar custom, rubbed her ever-growing baby bump. The Charlotte or Daniel one.

Chapter Nine:

For those of you lucky enough to have been through a pregnancy, and I am talking to men here, you would probably agree with me that the final days, awaiting the moment, are the longest and most boring of all. All preparations are in place. We have been over and over the emergency 'It's on its way' plan for when it all kicks off. I even had a heart-to-heart with Bonnie, explaining she had a little brother or sister coming soon, and she would have to calm the heck down. I think she took it on board.

I would go to work, as usual, leaving Dawn to potter slowly around the house. I would come home and cook a healthy meal for her, all colourful and tasteless. I did try to embrace the broccoli and chickpeas, but I had made enough sacrifices drinking Morrisons' non-alcoholic Chardonnay for the past six months so I sampled the delights of different pies instead, with chips, and gravy.

Dawn had become, quite rightly, a bit grumpy and fed up. Getting up from the sofa was a chore and I would try to entertain her with quips like 'now you know what it's like; my back has made me feel like that for years', and similar comments. To her credit though, she wouldn't engage, and just ignored me. I blame Derek Trotter. One of my favourite comedy memories is the Only Fools and Horses episode when Raquel gave birth. I have never laughed, or cried, as much as watching this exquisite episode. From Del Boy taking huge gulps of gas in the hospital to the final moving scene, holding his son to the clear night sky, while reciting his beautiful monologue. I wanted to recreate the whole darn thing. To make Dawn laugh through the birth and to have my own emotional speech at the end.

My memory of the actual day, before the momentous moment, is a little bit hazy. It was certainly a Saturday and I do remember arguing with Dawn with regards to taking Bonnie for a walk. She had started to feel some mild contractions but they were hours apart so she was adamant that taking the dog around the block would be perfectly okay. I, on the other hand, was not so sure and was digging my size elevens in. Of course, I took her in the end, but it was in a world record time that even Usain Bolt would have been proud of. Poor Bonnie never stopped once and just dribbled on the pavement, like a slobby maze, all the way around. On my return, I couldn't keep still. Whilst Dawn was lying on the sofa, mentally counting minutes, I was up and down like a Mr Motivator workout. I would sit and stroke her hair to be told to 'do one'. I would then go and make a coffee; stand and watch her, then sit back down and stroke her amazingly beautiful bump. She would, once more, tell me to 'do one'.

At about 4 pm on Saturday 7th April 2001, Dawn announced that she thought it was time she made her way to the hospital. To relieve any stress she may be feeling, or quite possibly my own, I ran around in circles, first in the living room and then out in the hallway and kitchen, arms in the air, shouting, "don't panic, don't panic" in a high-pitched Duncan Norvelle voice.

Back in the lounge, feeling pleased with myself, I was greeted with a cold stare, followed by a 'shut up' and get the car ready'. I decided to curb the jokes for a while and just quietly support my darling partner. I glanced for a final time at our checklist, loaded the emergency bag and waited at the front door. And waited. Feeling a little frustrated, I stomped into the living room to find Dawn still lying on the sofa.

"All ready, my love," I said in the calmest voice I could muster. "Your carriage awaits you."

"I think I am going to struggle to get to the car. Can you carry me?" She was looking at me with a vulnerability in her eyes.

"You are kidding! I can't lift you into the bloody car. Christ, I couldn't have lifted you pre-child. You have no idea the nightmares I have, thinking that you might ask me to carry you over the threshold, if we ever got married, that is."

"I do hope you are not suggesting I am too heavy without a baby stuck up my belly," she smiled. "Is that a proposal by the way?"

"Not now, Dawn. Bigger fish to fry. Baby to be born and all that. You are just big-boned, that's all. Cracking bones, though."

She looked at me dubiously.

"Can you at least try and lift me? I am just a bit worried that my legs will wobble."

I cannot possibly describe the next few minutes. It was hands and legs in all sorts of places as I tried to position Dawn so that I could lift her. Basically, a pregnancy version of Twister. I attempted a fireman's lift, but before you start screaming at the page, I soon realised this was not the smartest move. All the while, Dawn was laughing loudly which was rather off-putting and annoying. There was a huge amount of huffing and puffing from yours truly, but she wasn't making too much of an effort to assist me.

"It doesn't help that you are pissing yourself and can't stay still," I said, rather exasperated. I stood back, my hands on my knees in exhaustion. Dawn put her hands down hard on the sofa and pushed herself up with ease.

"Two of us can play at trying to be funny and cracking jokes," she said, as she calmly walked out of the living room.

The hospital was a twenty-minute drive through the late traffic, so we settled down, but my nerves and anticipation were growing by the second. I could feel a knot building in my stomach; a strangely pleasant feeling, like an actor about to go on stage or a player psyching themselves up for a cup final. We didn't say much to each other, both deep in thought at what was about to happen, and the change in our lives forever. 'What took you so long?' by Emma Bunton was playing on the radio, which seemed applicable for the moment, even if I did have a momentary flashback to the past. I glanced over at Dawn with a reassuring smile and she instinctively put her hand on my thigh and squeezed it gently.

My God, hospitals are depressing. Pulling up outside, the grey concrete block stares at you with sadness and a persona that asks, 'Do you really want to come in here?' I presume that this look is deliberate but, as I helped Dawn out of the car, I did ponder whether they could be bright, funky, and full of colour. For our visit that would be in keeping with how we were feeling, but it might also work for the harrowing times when a hospital is required, and colour might just give some people a miniscule of relief from what was to come.

As we approached the main entrance Dawn stopped and turned towards me.

"I love you," she said, as she kissed me softly on the lips. "Don't forget, when we leave here there will be three of us."

What a thought. What a feeling. I squeezed her hand as we went through the automatic doors as a couple for the last time.

Chapter Ten:

After the formalities of checking in, Dawn settled down in her room for the duration, however long that might be. One of the nurses asked if a cup of tea would be in order and I couldn't resist.

"Yes please, and I think Dawn wouldn't mind one either," which was straight out of the Del Boy script.

Whilst the nurse gave me a pitying smile, Dawn stared at me with contempt. She unpacked her bag and whilst the essentials of fresh pyjamas, toothbrush, etc. were expected, the bright yellow tennis ball that Bonnie must have dropped in was not, but it gave us a reassuring feeling and a seal of approval from our beloved pooch. I am not sure that the dozen packets of pickled onion Space Raiders which I had put in the bottom were welcome, but she had been munching them by the barrel-load for the past few months, so I thought they would be of comfort through the long hours ahead. Not so.

"Why the hell have you packed these?" she asked, pulling bag after bag out.

"I thought they would be comforting for you. I know you love them, so I thought I would surprise you."

"I am having a bloody baby. I can't be seen with hundreds of aliens in my mouth. I need some fruit so that the nurses think I am a healthy mum-to-be."

It was an interesting observation but not one I believed the midwife would give a flying saucer about, but I was here to please, not annoy.

"I will nip out and get you some bananas and apples in a while. That should prevent them from chucking you out. Shall we hide the Raiders or will you be sneaking a packet between your cheeks when you frequent the ladies room?"

Dawn shook her head. "Don't be a sarcastic knob."

It was a truly strange experience. Nothing happened for hours. Dawn would have a little nap and then read the couple of books she had packed. She alternated between Bridget Jones, which I approved of wholeheartedly, and Harry Potter which, and I am sorry if I upset any of you, is just not my cup of tea. I, of course, had packed sod all, so I sat in the battered chair which was uncannily like Ronnie Corbett's when he did his monologues, and then would wander out into the corridor just to see some movement and life.

It took me a couple of hours to notice that there was a television in our room. It was up on the wall, right in the corner, and after a period of swearing, I located the remote and settled down to watch the delights of Saturday night TV.

I enjoyed Match of the Day and, thankfully, a certain person didn't make an appearance. I'm not sure that Dawn was appreciative, but she was very restrained during this crucial hour and a half, and I only detected a loud sigh on a handful of occasions. On its conclusion, I decided that I should nip home and take Bonnie out for a quick walk and grab some fruit for a pointless static display that would prove our caring parenthood.

A quick check with the experts and mum-to-be that nothing was about to happen, and I was away, out of the mundane existence of the last five hours. It is odd, but the excitement starts to wane while you are waiting. I know it is the calm before the storm, but you work yourself up with all sorts of emotions as you arrive but then nothing. Zilch. The boredom is excruciating. A selfish statement, granted, but from a father's perspective the giddiness disappears for a while and I actually felt resentment that I was being put through this delay.

Bonnie, as always, was pleased to see me and we made our way out into the back garden. It was such a beautiful, clear night and no outside lights were needed as she galloped away, fetching the ball over and over again, as I sat inhaling the starry night. I was tired but it was emotional fatigue. Of course, my state was ridiculous in the context of what Dawn was going through. Her feelings and worries were acute, but you can't help your own feelings, however much you metaphorically slap yourself around the face. Back inside the warm house, I lay on the sofa where Bonnie joined me, snuggling down by my feet, all curled up. I will just have five minutes, I thought to myself, and then head back to the hospital.

I woke up, startled. Disorientation was palpable. You know the feeling. No idea where you are, who you are, what day or time it is. Just for that split second. I sat up urgently, trying to focus on the clock on the fireplace. It was 3.10 am. My next thought was to locate my Blackberry, all the time trying to work out how long I had been asleep and how lengthy my absence had been from Dawn's side.

It worked out at just a shade over three hours and my stomach churned as I picked my phone up to see how many calls or messages I had missed. I had a sudden sinking feeling that I had missed the birth of our child. I remember feeling tears roll down my cheeks as I clicked the button to wake the technology up. Nothing. Not one notification. The sense of relief, coupled with a back-to-normal mode, was extraordinary. It was like the past few minutes had never existed. The emergency thoughts I had, of always living with the memory of not being there, squeezing Dawn's hand, pretending to suck on the gas 'Del Boy style', and shouting, "Go on girl, give it some welly," completely disappeared. I still had the opportunity to do all of these things as I grabbed my keys, gave Bonnie a kiss, and jumped back into my car.

"Where the hell have you been?"

Dawn was sitting bolt upright, wide-eyed and looking as fresh as the morning that would soon be upon us.

"Sorry. I got a bit waylaid with Bonnie, walking, a bit of tidying," I lied, "but I had my phone glued to my hand so I knew nothing was happening and I thought a bit of peace and quiet from me would be helpful. You could get some sleep without distractions."

"Aw. Thank you. I did drift off for a while. You must be shattered. Why don't you get a bit of shut-eye in the chair? I am sure we will wake you if needed."

"No. I'm fine. I feel wide awake. Must be the adrenalin."

I can hear some of you yelling 'fibber' and others whispering 'wise move', but there was no point in telling the truth at this point and my little white lie made her feel loved and cared for. That was what mattered. No need for soaring blood pressure at this late stage.

The clock on the far wall seemed to be moving ever so slowly. I am sure I only glanced at it every half-hour, but the bloody thing had only moved a few minutes. It was also getting on my nerves that this timepiece, which had probably been put up in the 1960s, with its dull white face and enormous black numbers, had a ticking noise louder than a joiner's hammer.

Dawn was getting more frequent contractions but nowhere near the timings to activate Operation Raquel. This one was named after Del Boy's girlfriend and was my suggestion. We had stumbled on naming any forthcoming big events with a title early on in our relationship. Childish I know, but we loved them. As you will recall, we had Operation Dogging, which was a huge success, but there were others, such as Operation Waite named after the extraordinary Terry Waite who was held captive in Beirut for four years. Whilst you might feel this is rather tasteless, I can promise you it was concocted with enormous respect and humility and was associated with visiting my mother for a week.

As the hammer whacked out another second and the time reached 5 am, I gingerly got up from my Ronnie Corbett throne and decided to stretch my legs. I checked with Dawn for any requirements but she was too busy eating her umpteenth pack of Space Raiders, so I ambled out into the corridor for a stroll. It was quiet as I walked down the long, dreary aisle. A couple of porters passed me and we nodded a respectful 'hello' to each other.

I looked out of the windows at the car park below as I continued on my way. A couple of nurses were next in sight, purposefully walking towards me, heading to help and support those in need. As they passed me, I smiled at them both. One didn't look at me at all but the other stopped momentarily, as though she was about to say something, but then just smiled back and carried on catching up with her colleague.

Something didn't feel right. Suddenly my brain was activating all sorts of strange thoughts, trying to tell me something, imploring me to think. And then it happened. My head settled on what it was desperately pressuring me to compute. I turned around abruptly and shouted back down the corridor.

"Louise? ... Lou?" The nurse stopped, turned around, and looked at me intently. A slow, tentative smile of recognition appeared from us both as she turned her body and slowly walked towards me.

Chapter Eleven:

The hospital corridor suddenly felt small and intimate. The nurse who was accompanying Louise had long gone, leaving the two of us standing, looking at each other. The silence was eery as the morning started to break. My head was a bit scrambled at this point. Not for any whimsical lost love, but just the situation in front of me. A past girlfriend who I nearly had a child with, had not seen for over twelve years, was now working at the local hospital where my current girlfriend was about to have my child. It was not an everyday occurrence so my confused state, in conjunction with a swathe of sadness, enveloped me momentarily. She hadn't changed much, which could have prompted me to add a joke, but that moment was not appropriate for humour.

"I thought it was you," I said, as calmly as possible. "As you passed, I was racking my brains. Sorry I didn't... What on earth are you doing here? Sorry, that is a daft question. I presume you are working here?"

We were facing each other, quite close, and it was that awkward moment with regards to whether we should be hugging like long-lost lovers, shaking hands like absent friends, or doing neither and taking up an uncomfortable posture. We were stuck at the last option.

"I have been here about a year," she replied cheerily. "I needed a change of scenery, a quieter life. A bit more sedate than London. What about you? Are you visiting? Or here for other matters?"

"Just visiting, thankfully."

Now what do I say? Do I just admit what I am here for? The joy I was about to experience. The delight we never went through. I decided just to bypass any detail.

"You just finishing a shift? Or just starting?"

"Just come on. Day shift. I'm a labour and delivery nurse."

As Humphrey Bogart once said, 'Of all the hospital joints in all the towns in all the world, she walks into mine', or something like that. You are probably mumbling about this becoming all too far-fetched. Worse than Bobby Ewing having a shower. Trust me, this is what happened. However, just because she was a delivery nurse did not mean she would be involved in the one I was about to have. The speed this particular labour was going, she would be long retired anyway.

"Who are you visiting? Hope they are okay?" Louise jerked me out of the 'FFS' thought process.

"A friend. My girlfriend, actually. She is trying to have a baby."

"Trying? I hope it's a bit more advanced than trying," Louise laughed. "It's fine you know. You can talk normally. You can be just you."

"Sorry. Just a bit shocked. Seeing you and…" I let the sentence drift. "I better get back. Went AWOL earlier on this morning and got away with it. Not sure I will a second time."

"Yes, of course. Might see you around and about. Good luck."

And with that, she turned on her heels and headed down the corridor towards the maternity unit. Suddenly she stopped and turned her head towards me.

"What's your girlfriend's name?"

"Dawn," I answered.

Louise glanced at a small clipboard that I hadn't noticed she was carrying.

"Dawn Walsh?" she asked, in a calm, clinical manner.

"Yes," I answered, all too ready for what was coming next.

"Excellent. She is one of mine. See you soon."

Far-fetched doesn't cover it at all.

I allowed enough time for Louise to disappear from view and then took a deep breath. I stared out of the window and gathered my thoughts. Once more my overactive brain had hundreds of little ideas swirling around. How was this going to play out? Should I go home, pretend the dog had a freak yachting accident so I couldn't be there for the birth? Do I urgently tell Dawn, who was about to deliver our baby, about the background of the said nurse? Maybe just wing it, say nothing and, as usual in my moments of crisis, just ignore what is in front of me.

I came to my senses and realised that I was overreacting. Louise was a professional. She was just doing her job. It was a long time ago. There was no way she was going to blurt out a 'Wow, this could have been me' or 'I'm so glad he stuck around and supported you and didn't just bugger off as he did with me'. I stretched my head back, shook it clear of ridiculous thoughts and set off back to the delivery room and to Dawn.

On entering our room there was activity. A couple of nurses were talking to Dawn and monitoring her. Louise was not one of them, which was a relief. I raced to the side of the bed and grabbed her hand, squeezing it tightly.

"I'm here D. I'm here."

She rubbed her fingers on my hand and smiled.

"I think it's on its way," she stated slightly breathlessly. "I have had an epidural to help with the pain and the contractions are coming thick and fast."

"What's an epidural?" I asked Dawn but looked at the nurses for clarification.

"Don't worry Mr Walsh, it just stops you from feeling pain in parts of your body."

I couldn't be arsed to correct the nurse on addressing me by Dawn's surname. It was easier for all concerned just to get on with the job in hand.

"I might ask for one of those once it's all over. My back gives me so much jip. Does it stop emotional pain too?" I joked, linking the injection to how I might be feeling once this was all over. Especially if Louise made an appearance.

"There is no drug to help with emotional pain, Mr Walsh." The nurse smiled. "Just honesty, talking and listening. That is the best medicine for that."

"I will bear that in mind. Thank you," I said, as I turned back towards Dawn who was staring at me, again with contempt.

"What are you going on about? Cut the quips, stop trying to be bloody Del Boy, and just hold my hand. I'm scared."

I won't go into the details of what happened in the next couple of hours. Firstly, because it would be extremely hard to articulate, especially as the person who was just holding a hand and stroking hair. And secondly because I have extraordinarily little recollection of the actual birth. I know I was there. I have a vague memory of being asked to cut the cord but otherwise, I am as 'Blankety Blank' as good old Terry Wogan. I have no idea why. Possibly it was the traumatic scene I was witnessing, even if the ending was the gift of a beautiful new-born to the world. It might be the case that I have erased any memory due to the suffering Dawn went through as she pushed, shouted, and swore her way to giving birth to our baby. It doesn't matter in the grand scheme of things. What matters is that at 7.29 am on Sunday 8th April 2001, our gorgeous, perfect daughter was born.

In the end, Louise never entered our room. It might have been the case that she was not needed, or that she was teasing me with the announcement that she would be in charge of the birth. To be honest, she could have been there the whole time as I wouldn't have had a 'Scooby Doo', but I am sure I would have remembered that bit. Would I ever see her again? Would our paths cross in this environment again? The former possibly, the latter highly unlikely.

For those of you who have not dropped off by now, and are still wading through this tale, you will remember the name we gave to our beautiful girl. You do, don't you? Just in case you haven't, and to stop you going back to chapter eight, we named her Charlotte, after establishing it was the only girls' name that yours truly had not had a crush on.

She weighed in at eight pounds nine ounces and her birth was the most extraordinary thing ever to happen to me. I was in awe of her. I was in a daze those first few hours. I would alternate between staring at and holding Charlotte and gazing with amazement and wonder at her mother.

This day was the start of the rest of my life and I couldn't wait for the journey to begin. I knew how lucky I was, to get this second chance, and that whatever happened from now on, this tiny wonder of the world would have more love than she could ever imagine.

Chapter Twelve:

The first twenty-four hours of fatherhood were a whirlwind. Phone calls and messages in and out to family and friends. My mum was ecstatic but did advise us that her time bringing up children was over. Whilst she looked forward to seeing Charlotte, she made it abundantly clear that until she was old enough to traipse around some castle or share a scenic train journey, seeing her only briefly was going to be the plan for a few years. She was certainly not going to be a hands-on grandma, which is understandable, given the amount of love and attention she bestowed on the three of us for so long. She must have been emotionally exhausted.

I was the first of Mum's children to have a child and it was a poignant moment when I informed my brother and sister about the good news. They were genuinely delighted and I was desperate to see them all but any such arrangements were put on hold whilst we adjusted to our new life and structure. Dawn had furnished me with a list of friends to contact and I waded my way through as many as possible. I had come to detest making phone calls, and talking to people for that matter, as my sales role included this most days and it was just so depressing and repetitive. This was different. These were joyous calls and I loved every single one of them.

The remainder of this Jack Bauer timeline was spent to-ing and fro-ing from the hospital, making sure Dawn and Charlotte were okay, going home to entertain Bonnie and shopping for any provisions requested. This mainly meant acquiring more fruit but it was beginning to stack up a bit by her bedside and whilst it looked like a healthy cubicle, it also resembled a Dave and Betty's market stall. We could have had a profitable little business going for a few days if we had scattered posters around the wards advertising our wares. I had even thought of a name. 'An Apple a day...' Marketing was never my strong point.

It was whilst I was leaving Dawn and Charlotte, for the third time, that I bumped into Louise in the corridor. I was so euphoric that any thoughts of sadness or regret towards her were non-existent.

"I missed you last night," I said cheerily. "I was hoping you would be in there with us."

It was a crass and insensitive comment.

"Really? I think if you had thought that through you would probably not say it again."

She was smiling in an understanding way, but it jolted me back from my self-centred jubilation.

"Christ. I am so sorry. Been in this intoxicating, emotional bubble since the birth. Had no thoughts of anything else, or anyone for a few hours. Apart from Mum and Daughter of course."

"It's okay. I'm used to it."

Her head moved left to right, contemplating.

"Used to most scenarios, I mean. This one is a bit different from normal but you can't let yourself think or be distracted from the job in hand. Thankfully I wasn't needed, so I concentrated on a few other mums-to-be. Congratulations by the way. A girl I believe?"

She leant up against the window in a dignified, relaxed posture.

"Thank you. Yes. A girl. Charlotte."

"That's a lovely name. Any middle name?"

"Blimey," I said, "that would take far too much debate. I won't bore you with the details of how the first name came about, but I don't think I could go through the same process for a second time."

She laughed and said, "Then I won't ask. She needs a middle name though. Girls should have one."

"As the delivery expert, I will take your advice on board and give it some thought."

We both laughed and the invisible awkwardness seemed to disappear by the second.

We stood and chatted for a few minutes. All rather bland and, as in some cases with Lou, clinical. I learnt that she owned a house on the other side of town from me. She had never married but had a long relationship that had recently ended. She was enjoying a quieter life and loved working at this hospital. She did look content and happy as she babbled away.

"Where are you off to?" Louise suddenly changed the subject. "Nappy hunting or similar?"

"No," I smiled, "whizzing home to check on the dog. She is feeling rather neglected. Like me. That's a joke by the way!"

She looked at me quizzically.

"I am just finishing my shift," she replied. "Fancy a walk in the park? You could give that dog some much-needed exercise and you can tell me all about Charlotte. Only if you want though. And if you have time?"

The request was a bit left-field, to be honest. This is where the brain acts at its stupidest. I was standing there telling myself not to get involved, that I loved Dawn, had a beautiful baby daughter less than 24 hours old. That I should let her down gently when all she had asked me to do was have a walk in the park. How arrogant was I? Why was my head telling me that she still fancied the boxer shorts off me, when the reality, if you could have seen us, was the complete opposite. She was just being kind and thoughtful. That's the male brain for you. Completely irrational and shallow.

"That would be lovely," I said genuinely. "It might be an hour by the time I have picked Bonnie up, if that's okay with you. Sabling Park? By the ice cream van? You know where that is, I presume?"

"Yes, I know. Perfect. I need to get out of this tunic anyway. See you soon then."

Louise walked purposefully down the corridor as I watched. I didn't feel anything. For me, it was a chance to talk properly, apologise and hopefully set my guilt free.

The sun was still shining brightly as I sat on a bench by the 'Ice Ice Baby' mobile van. It has to be said that the mature man conjuring up the Mr Whippy was a good likeness to Vanilla Ice, albeit a rather mature and slightly wider version. The kids wouldn't have had a clue, of course, but us adults would have had a wry smile. It was an unseasonably warm afternoon and the play areas were busy, as were the skateboarding ramps, and the mix of ages between the two had me whimsically thinking into the future and the times I would be spending with Charlotte.

Bonnie was as alert as ever, waiting for the odd iced blob that would land at her feet from passers-by. I looked to my left and Louise was heading towards me in a lovely bright floral dress that made her look much younger than her thirty years. I could see that she was smiling, and, for the first time, I didn't see my hero, Peter Beardsley, in her at all. I hadn't noticed at the hospital, but she had grown out of that lookalike face and just had a lovely, caring profile.

She sat down next to me, giving Bonnie's ears a ruffle.

"She is gorgeous. Look at those grey whiskers. How old is she?"

"Not far off hitting her seventh birthday," I replied. "She is a bit of a rock for me. Helped me through one or two scrapes."

"I'm sure she has. I wish I could have one. Not a scrape, a dog I mean, but with my job…"

She gazed into the distance.

"Maybe one day."

"Are you okay?" I asked as Louise continued to gaze, mostly towards the skateboarding area.

"Yes. I'm fine. Sorry. It's very warm."

She waved her hand in front of her face.

"I'm glad we could get some time together. It's been a long time," she stopped mid-sentence, and as I looked at her and waited for her to finish, we were interrupted by two boys, with skateboards in hand.

"Mum, can I go with Nick to McDonald's? His dad says he will take us and drop me home later."

The boy, dressed smartly in a Gorillaz T-shirt and shorts, was talking directly to Louise, while the second boy, presumably Nick, was nonchalantly posing, jeans torn to shreds, with hair like Doc from Back to the Future.

"Yes okay," Louise replied, "but home by 6.30 pm, please. I will be back by then."

"Is that your final answer?" replied the boy, in a sort of Chris Tarrant piss-take. And then they were gone. Hurtling across the park towards the cars.

I was trying to compute what I had just witnessed. It didn't help that I still had an image of Chris Tarrant in my head. Did that boy really just call her what I thought he had?

"Did he just call you Mum?" I stuttered.

Louise stopped me in my verbal tracks. Her fingers went over my lips as she moved closer to me. Her eyes locked into mine.

"He did," she said softly. "He is called Peter, and he is your son."

Chapter Thirteen:

I finally stopped, deep in the woodlands. I was bent over double, desperately trying to bring my heart rate down as the gasps for breath slowly subsided. I could have run in any direction, but the trees and solace seemed to be a magnet as I set off as fast as I could.

Why did I run? It's a darn good question, with no answer I'm afraid. Maybe I was just running away from my past or running headlong back into my future with Dawn and Charlotte. I stood up and stretched as the late sunshine peaked through the trees. It was eerily quiet, and I realised I had strayed from the main path, leaving a destruction of branches and bushes behind me. I was on my own, only accompanied by the beautiful chirps of the birds above and a few bewildered squirrels scurrying in all directions to the safety of the untreated timber.

How would you have dealt with the revelation I had just heard? You would probably have stayed put and found out what the bloody hell had happened all those years ago, and you would have been right. That was my thought process now, but I had no idea where I was and how to get back to Louise pronto and ask her questions like Bob Monkhouse in a quick-fire game show. I tried to get my bearings and managed to spot some children, in the distance, bobbing up and down at pace, which could only be the skateboarding ramp. The apparatus where my newly-announced son had arrived from.

I headed slowly towards my destination and hoped Louise was still there. I tried to follow the same route back, which was easier than I thought looking at the devastation I had caused coming the other way. So many emotions were battling each other for prominence in my head. The main one was the fact that I had a twelve-year-old son. All those years when I thought he would never have the opportunity of life. That a decision by a couple of kids had robbed him of his creation. The irony of Louise calling him Peter kept what little humour I had left bubbling away in the background, as I waded my way through the brambles.

The first thoughts I processed were ones of anger. Why had she not told me before? Why had she not got in touch, before or after she changed her mind? These subsided very quickly when I remembered what an arsehole I had been. My indifference when she first told me, and my desperation to get the hell out of there and back to the comfort of my sad little existence, meant she owed me nothing. Further thoughts concentrated on what, if any, involvement she now wanted me to have, and then finally thoughts turned to Dawn. She had no knowledge of any of this. How could I tell her now? She had just given birth to our wonderful daughter and was so happy. A life fulfilled. How could I destroy that?

As I re-entered the park, looking like an extra from The Blair Witch Project, I finally realised what a self-centred dickhead I was. Like an actor playing a role, but in real life. Plotting a route that only served one person. Me. It was now blindingly obvious that my relationships were always on my terms. To fit my agenda.

Louise had given me the thrill of the bright lights of London but as soon as responsibility appeared, I was off, faster than Wacky Races. Susan had helped me deal with my loneliness at the time and, whilst the horrific violence I had occasionally endured excused me for the way I treated her, I was confident that I would still be with her if she had still served a purpose and Dawn had not come into my life. And now the realisation struck me that I was still doing it.

Don't get me wrong. I loved Dawn, but was it a love based on an escape route from Susan? A love that grew and was now cemented by the arrival of our daughter? I felt crestfallen that she, or my family for that matter, didn't know anything meaningful about me. About my past. My anguish. Painful burdens carried all on my own. None of them knew me. Not properly. How much better as a person might I have been if I had opened up and got help?

The park was much quieter now as I approached the bench that I had taken flight from a while ago. Louise was still sitting in the same spot, as I sat down next to her, this time slightly further apart. Thankfully, she had hold of Bonnie's lead and I was welcomed, enthusiastically, by at least one female. I was determined to listen and work through this together, not just from my own selfish perspective.

"I'm sorry I bolted," I began. "I hadn't had my run today and suddenly remembered."

I was hoping my attempt at a joke would soothe the charged atmosphere between the two of us.

"That's okay. I am glad you are just running now and not taking a train."

Not a great start, I thought to myself, but it was thoroughly deserved.

I was trying to think of the right words for the questions I wanted answering urgently, but Louise interrupted my thoughts.

"I should tell you what happened, shouldn't I?" she said calmly.

"Yes please," I replied quietly.

"When you left that night," she began, "I remember lying on my bed. I promise you, at that exact moment, I wasn't thinking of having Peter. I just stared at the ceiling, at that awful pink lampshade. It was swaying with the draught and I just started to think."

She paused momentarily.

"Then I started to imagine a normal life. One with children, one that had me falling in love, doing normal things, and not just the career that had consumed me since I was a little girl. Then a jolt, a realisation that a new life was growing inside me. That comprehension changes you."

Her head bowed as I waited for her to continue, the arrival of Vanilla Ice cream man sweeping the rubbish in our vicinity, seemingly interrupting her.

"Why didn't you tell me?" I asked. "You could have got in touch."

She looked at me contemptuously.

"Would you have answered if I had called? I think we both know how you felt about the situation. Don't kid yourself now with hindsight. Let's not go there."

She looked at me, steely-eyed.

"You're right," I admitted. "I probably wouldn't have even taken your call. I have never told anyone. Not Dawn, not my family."

I hurriedly moved the discussion on.

"Does he know about me? Did he know who I was this afternoon?"

I'm not sure how I would have reacted, whatever the answer happened to be, but I suppose I was hankering for some clarity.

"No, and No," was her short answer. "He doesn't know who his dad is. He has asked a couple of times and I have always told him it was a brief relationship and that I had no idea where he was. Kind of true though, don't you think?"

"I suppose so. I'm not quite sure how I feel about that."

"Your feelings don't come into it," she continued, in a curt manner, reminiscent of a different time. "That is how I dealt with it. It would have stayed that way too if I hadn't bumped into you. It might still stay that way. I haven't decided yet."

She looked at me, trying to gauge my reaction, but I didn't have one.

Vanilla Ice cream man was still in the vicinity, slowly bending down, picking up the remnants of litter strewn on the path and grass. He was suddenly standing in front of us, leaning on his brush.

"I couldn't help overhearing," he began in a higher-pitched voice that was unexpected, given his stature, "but I went through something similar myself."

It is at these moments when you should say what you are thinking. 'Bugger off' would be reasonable in the circumstances, but we don't do we? Most of us default to politeness.

"I'm sorry," I said, hardly believing what was coming out of my mouth, "that must have been awful for you."

"Well, yes it was," he continued, "although when I say similar, it's not quite what you two are talking about. You see my wife left me about two years ago. She had an affair with one of my rivals. He had a better van, you see. Better places to trade too, you see. Never saw it coming. They used to do it in his van. We could have done that too, but I added an extra-long freezer so no space, you see."

You see? I knew I should have told him to bugger off.

Louise looked at me, her expression perplexed. She was possibly imagining, as I was, if it was practicable to make love with or without the additional cold storage, but it was far more likely that she was bewildered that his story was even remotely similar to our situation.

"I presume you have frozen her out then?" I said, with the saddest look I could muster. In my book, sarcasm is the highest form of wit, although Vanilla Ice didn't get it. Shame.

"Oh no," he blathered on, "we still talk, you see…"

Louise, keeping heroically calm, interrupted.

"It must have been awful for you," she said quietly, "but, and this is not being disrespectful, could you please just FUCK OFF!"

The last two words boomed out across the park and woodlands. People stopped whatever they were doing and stared in our general direction. I am sure I saw a couple of squirrels shaking their heads in a nearby tree.

Vanilla Ice looked dejected.

"I was only trying to help, you see," he said hurtfully. "Don't know why I bother."

We were both looking at him, our mouths slightly ajar, waiting for him to finish with 'you see' again, but he nonchalantly thrust the sweeping brush onto the back of his shoulders and gradually meandered towards his van.

I turned back towards Louise, shaking my head. I was eager to continue where we had left off, but she was now looking at her phone.

"Sorry," she said hurriedly, "I need to go. A friend wants to see me back at the hospital and then I need to get home."

She passed me the dog lead; Bonnie attached. Lou stood up, adjusted her dress, ready to leave.

"We need to talk, Lou. We need to sort this out."

She smiled sympathetically.

"You never sort things out though, do you? You never talk, not properly. Give me some time, please. I will sort it out. I promise."

And with that last cryptic sentence, she leant down, kissed my cheek, and walked purposefully in the direction of the car park.

Chapter Fourteen:

Perched on a rickety old bar stool in the kitchen, I sipped a small glass of chilled Chardonnay. The first for many months. I wanted to guzzle it, and preferably in a pint pot, but I was fully aware that I would soon be heading back to visit Dawn and our precious new-born. Bonnie lay at my feet, twitching in her sleep; the last few hours had taken their toll. A bit like her owner then.

I sat there and tried to write a script in my head. How I was going to confess all to Dawn. I now had a son, she had a stepson and in addition, our daughter had a brother. Tricky when you say it like that. I do remember feeling a sense of calmness though. As though years of pent-up secrets were about to drift upwards like smoke finally escaping an unblocked chimney.

The issue, in reality, wasn't that I had another child. I suppose that could happen to any man, within reason. It was the events surrounding this sudden announcement. What had happened, what really happened, and how on earth I had never thought to tell her, especially on that notorious evening when we found out she was pregnant, and the aftermath. Prior to that, I should have told her when we had those highly charged, flirty evenings in the pub. Before we were an actual couple. She could have known all about Louise then. And the unvarnished truth with regards to my relationship with Susan. Imagine how much difference that would make now?

This is certainly not a self-help book but take my advice on this one. Help yourself and be honest early. Get those rattling skeletons scattered out on to the floor. Easier to tidy up when there are not so many.

I put on a fresh shirt and trousers. I was dressed head to foot in white, like Tom Cruise in A Few Good Men, without the shiny gold buttons. Before you start criticising my wardrobe, there was a method in my madness. The nurses had quietly advised me to wear something lighter in colour. Something to do with babies' sick. I thought I would take it to the extreme and hopefully get a laugh or two. I still desperately wanted to deliver my version of the Del Boy birth scene. I know. Childish behaviour, as always. I gave Bonnie a shake of the paw so as not to discolour my pristine outfit and headed once again to the hospital, where my future destiny would be decided.

As I got out of my car, I realised that I had not checked my phone for some time. Thankfully, there was nothing from Dawn but there were a few missed calls. A couple from my brother and one from my sister. A bit odd I thought, as I strolled towards the main entrance. They would have to wait though, as more important events were about to take place.

It seemed busier than usual as the evening sunshine began to dip. A couple of ambulances were blocking my path to the doorway so I walked the long way round before seeing the automatic doors. A few people were milling around, dragging on cigarettes, and then I spotted what looked like my brother Craig. Yep, it was him. Standing next to him was my mum. Next to her, my sister, Jess. Auntie June from Whitby was also in attendance, as was Auntie Beryl from Northampton. I couldn't make up my mind what they all looked like, just loitering outside. The Addams Family would have been a good starting point.

"Surprise!" My mum screamed as she advanced towards me. Surprise indeed. And one I could have done without.

There followed the usual family hugs, my mother insistent on kissing both my cheeks. 'Like the Spanish', as she always said on welcoming occasions. Then followed a flurry of small talk between us all. I should have been ecstatic and overwhelmed that my lovely family had organised this open-mouthed moment, but I wasn't. My future life was all that consumed me.

"It really is brilliant you have done this," I said, a touch ingeniously. "I can't believe you have driven miles to congratulate me. Sorry, I mean us, don't I?" I laughed, "but I don't think D is ready to see anyone yet. She is very tired."

"Nonsense," Mum replied, in her best female Don Corleone voice. "She is on her way down now with the baby. We are meeting in the café."

She had a huge beam across her face. I bet Dawn hadn't. My guess was that she would be fuming at the lot of us, but especially me for not being around to head them off at the pass. She hadn't even acquired twenty-four hours as a spanking new mother, and yet there she was, being asked to parade herself in front of my family, like something out of a P T Barnum attraction.

We walked through reception and waited in the corridor by the café. The lifts were in front of us and every time my family heard a 'ping' and the doors opened, there was an expectant chatter and then a sigh of disappointment as some unwell soul exited, which was a bit disrespectful, in all honesty. I stood in silence. I just wanted to be on my own with Dawn. To hold her. My brother, Craig, noticed my expression and sidled over.

"You okay, Kitten?" he asked. My nickname. You can't help a tag name afforded to you. Mine was given to me by my fellow teammates at the local football club when I was younger. Most goalkeepers are named The Cat for their agility between the posts. I was not very agile. You can work out the rest for yourselves.

"I'm great, Craig," I lied. "Great, but bloody tired."

"I bet you are. Bloody proud of you. Can't believe you are a dad. Didn't think you had it in you!"

He punched me on the shoulder in a playful way, grinning from ear to ear. I wanted to reply that he was actually twelve years late. As was I.

Finally, another 'ping' reverberated around the corridor and the doors opened. Dawn was sitting in a wheelchair, with a hospital porter behind her, directing proceedings. As she was pushed into the corridor, I could see Charlotte, wrapped in a cream blanket. She had a tiny bobble hat covering most of her head and her fragile body was nuzzled in her mother's chest. Thankfully, she was fast asleep. She looked gorgeous, unlike her mother, who looked like Worzel Gummidge. This was understandable, given the short notice she must have received for this public show, but as I looked at her, I suddenly loved her even more. Properly. In her own right. Firstly, however dishevelled her appearance was, she looked stunning. And secondly, she had made this effort for my family, without knowing I was going to be there. That was some affection to muster. Just for me. I didn't deserve her I thought as she came towards me, but one day I would.

"Bloody hell, it's Lord Lucan," she said cheerily. "Don't tell me. Walking Bonnie again?"

Her sarcasm was cutting but I relished it. It's how we operated as a couple. I would have said something similar if the roles had been reserved.

"Sorry D," I replied, leaning down, and giving her a gentle kiss. "I did tidy the house too."

Dawn stared at me cheekily. "I can't wait to go home. The house must be like a ruddy show home with all the cleaning it's had."

My mother was next to approach.

"Congratulations Dawn."

She leaned in to kiss her on the cheek. Mum then held her head and turned it to the right. A kiss on the other cheek followed.

"Two kisses dear. Like the Spanish."

The next few minutes were a blizzard of kisses and congratulations. There was a huge amount of cooing, gentle prodding, and warmth towards the new mum, but especially the new addition to our family. I let them all have their turn and then gently cajoled them away, ushering them towards the exit. The hospital porter prepared to take Dawn back to the ward.

"I will just ensure that they have left the premises," I said jokingly, still getting the family together like a human sheepdog trial, "and then I will come up for a chat."

"Yes okay," she replied. "Look forward to that. Very much."

And with that, she was back in the lift.

I hugged my family one by one. Each was a tad too long but sincere from both sides. It was wonderful to see them however much I wish they hadn't come. I waved them into the distance, took a deep breath, and headed towards the lift. It was confession time.

Chapter Fifteen:

Ward 14 was eerily quiet. Apart from myself and Dawn, with baby Charlotte sleeping peacefully in her crib, there were just a couple of other new mothers discreetly enjoying their fresh little bundles of joy. I pulled the curtains across, so we had the privacy of our own cubicle, and sat down on one of those uncomfortable chairs that hospitals put there deliberately so you don't outstay your visiting time.

Dawn was sitting up, a bundle of pillows propping her comfortably. Her Worzel Gummidge look had calmed down a bit and she was sipping a cup of tea. I cursed under my breath at missing out on a hot cuppa. My mouth was parched. Actually, it was scorched, like a moth to a flame as I readied myself for confession and not in a Father Ted way. She was looking at me in a relaxed, calm way. Of course, this was normal but when you know you are about to say something that will turn their world upside down, somehow you expect their expression to be already ahead of you. Odd but true. I didn't clear my throat. I couldn't.

"How are you doing?" I asked as a gentle opener. "How's that magical daughter of ours doing?"

"I'm good, thanks. A bit tired and ready for a hell of a sleep. She's doing great. She's so quiet. No trouble at all. Yet anyway," she smiled lovingly.

"I need to tell you something D. I should have told you before. Right at the beginning when we met."

I was stumbling over my sentences and leant forward to grab her hand.

"Should have talked about it sooner. Never knew how to."

Dawn squeezed my hand.

"You're rambling and not making any sense. Slow down, take your time. I am listening."

"It's hard," I continued. "Maybe you should watch the film Secrets and Lies first and then come back to me. Christ, D, I can't say what I need to say."

I shook my head and rested it on our entwined hands. She put her fingers under my chin and lifted my head back up. Her eyes were full of empathy.

"Let me help you," she said softly. "I know you have a son. His name is Peter and I understand that you didn't know."

My reaction was mixed. Huge relief that this immense burden was suddenly lifted without me uttering a single syllable on the subject. Yet bewilderment as to how she knew.

"How?" I asked in shock. "How did you know?"

Dawn sat back, still gripping my hand.

"Louise told me."

She cupped my face delicately.

"She told me everything."

"How?" I replied in disbelief. "Why? And, just in case I have missed any out, when?"

I was still shaking my head, perplexed. That was my secret. Mine to share as I saw fit. Rather hypocritical though seeing as I never saw fit. Ever.

"She came to see me. Just before your family arrived with their Cilla Black impression."

She smiled at her own joke and continued.

"We had a long chat. About you. About Peter and Charlotte. I'm glad she did. Makes life easier."

"I still don't understand," I complained. "Why would she do that? What gives her the right to tell you my secret?"

As the words came out of my mouth, I could hear how preposterous they sounded.

"Well quite," she responded. "You don't know why? Really? Maybe she knew you better than you thought? She decided to take matters into her own hands when you confessed to not telling anyone about her. About what had happened. She thought you would never tell me. Not out of malice by the way. Just that you never talk. Properly. Sound familiar?"

The curtains twitched behind me and I imagined Vanilla Ice cream man popping his head through and interrupting with 'I couldn't help overhearing' followed by 'you see', but thankfully it was just one of the nurses checking in. Louise was right of course. I was not totally sure that I would have told her. I was trying to, but the words just wouldn't come.

"I knew something," she continued. "I knew something was bothering you. Niggling away."

"In what way?"

"I'm not sure. I remember you crying when we watched that film, Alfie. I did think it was odd. You tried to hide it, but I saw you."

"I can't remember," I lied.

"You must do. I was drooling over Jude Law the whole time."

"Not much of a reminder D. You dribble at most men on the TV. You even said Christopher Lloyd was fit when we were watching Back to the Future."

We both smiled, our hands still entwined tightly.

What followed was a detailed explanation of Louise's visit. She told Dawn what had happened all those years ago and why she had not told me about her change of heart. That she mustn't blame me and that, although it was a shock for both Dawn and me, she was not to let it get in the way of the two of us and, more importantly, Charlotte. They agreed it didn't change anything between the two of us and our new family. I sat and listened intently. I was in awe of them both. Louise for having the courage to take the proverbial bull by the horns, and Dawn for her maturity to process this unexpected announcement and take it in her stride, deciding it would change our lives, but not our life.

When she had finally finished, I shook my head slowly.

"I don't deserve you, I really don't."

"Don't be silly, daft sod," she said affectionately. "It might have been a bit different if you had known all along and had been paying maintenance all of his life. But you didn't and I think you have suffered enough in your own little world. Don't you?"

It was hard to disagree with that last sentence and it prompted me to want to unburden my other suffering. Dawn had opened the gates of my emotions and for once I was going to drive straight through them.

Charlotte had woken up and I found myself pulling funny faces at her as I rocked her in my arms. She was so fragile but mesmerising to look at. I sang a few lines from Teenage Dirtbag which was a bit close to the past.

"I also need to come clean about Susan," I suddenly blurted out, with Charlotte still swaying gently in my grasp.

Dawn stared at me. A look of pure panic in her eyes.

"What's she got?" she shouted rather loudly. "Bloody triplets?"

"Keep it down, will you, please." I put a half-hearted hand towards her mouth. "You will scare the shit out of Charlotte and those poor mothers trying to get some sleep. Of course, she hasn't got triplets. Well, she might have now for all I know but nothing to do with me if she has. God help them if she has. God help the father for that matter."

"What are you babbling on about? Have you had any type of child with her or not?"

"NO," I shouted back, and it was her turn for the hand-to-mouth manoeuvre.

I steadied myself, trying to think of the right description.

"She hurt me," I began, "physically. She punched and beat me. Sometimes she literally battered me." I fell silent as I remembered the country hotel.

I could see that Dawn was trying to process this revelation. Woman-on-man domestic abuse is not easy to comprehend. It was one of the main reasons I hadn't told anyone. I imagined everyone would look at me with incredulity or suspicion. I knew she wasn't thinking down those lines. I thought she was rewinding. To collect any clues.

"Is that why you never told her? That you were leaving, I mean."

I knew it. She does like a good pause and rewind.

"Why didn't you tell me?"

"I couldn't at first," I replied, as I passed Charlotte over, my arms numb. "I didn't know you well enough and you were so confident and, I suppose, a bit loud. You probably wouldn't have believed me or thought I was a bit of a wimp."

"Why would I think that?"

"I know now that you wouldn't have. But at the time. Then we just carried on and it didn't seem important anymore."

"But it is important, isn't it? Otherwise, you wouldn't be telling me now. It's always been important to you. It always will be. And it should be too."

We spent the next half hour talking it through. Mostly me, describing in detail some of the uncomfortable situations I had faced. How sometimes it was the unexpected that was worse than the expected. Dawn listened, touching, and stroking my hands and face, reassuring me that she was involved now and that I wasn't on my own anymore. When I finally paused for breath, Dawn put Charlotte back in her crib asleep and took me into her arms, holding me as though she never wanted to let go.

We were both emotionally exhausted as darkness fell. A decision was made that I should go and check on our pristine showroom home and get some sleep. There was a fresh feeling to the relationship, and it was a lovely warm, fuzzy emotion. I kissed Dawn's forehead as I got up to leave.

"Can I ask you something?" I said, turning back from the curtained exit.

She nodded with a hint of exhaustion.

"Did Louise say anything about meeting Peter? Either me or both of us?"

"No, she didn't. We never got that far. Let the dust settle and see what happens. It has to be her decision. You understand that don't you?"

"Yes, I know. Just wondered, that's all."

"Whatever happens," she said softly, "we will be together to deal with it. Now go and get some sleep."

I smiled, ready to leave a second time.

"Oh, I nearly forgot," Dawn said, ushering me back. "Apparently, girls should always have a middle name. A nurse told me."

"That's funny. A nurse told me that too, not so long ago," I replied.

"Don't forget to give Charlotte Louise a kiss then, before you bugger off."

As I wondered down the long corridor, a smile of relief was etched on my face but I also had a huge amount of baggage swirling around my brain. This tale of one unexpected birth was in reality a story of two unexpected ones, but I am sure you will agree with me that I couldn't have used that as a title. It would have ruined the climax.

I finally made it to my car and sat, engine off, staring through the fly massacre on my windscreen. The long walk from saying goodbye to Dawn and Charlotte, to arriving at my vehicle had cleared my mind of some things, and one of them was to be decisive with something that had been niggling away for the past few months. And that was to marry Dawn. I loved her very much and we had been through so much together, primarily this one unexpected birth.

One Hapless Wedding

Chapter One:

How many weddings have you been to? It's hard to put a number on it when you start to think about it. There are your own, of course, and, for a few, that could be four or five marriages in these modern times. Then there are the occasions when you might have had the honour of being a best man, maid of honour, bridesmaid or usher. Next on the list is being lucky enough to be invited as a guest to someone's special day, through family or close friends.

For the purposes of this collective calculation, I will also accept evening reception invites. You know the ones I mean. Not classed as close enough to the adorable couple for the main event but acceptable enough to add to the newlyweds' stack of presents. I am not a fan of this type of invite. You are an afterthought. The overspill of people they think they had better invite so they don't have to explain why you didn't make the important cut.

I nearly forgot. Finally, there are the weddings you may have attended as a child, if you can remember, that is. You personally hadn't been invited of course; it just so happened that you belonged to someone who had. I am sure when you add them all up you will be shocked at the number of ceremonies you have attended. How much cheap fizz or sherry you have consumed, even as a young boy or girl. Some will live long in the memory, that you still discuss to this day, but not always for the right reasons. There will be others that you have a vague recollection of, but were so dreary and boring, that you have to rack your brains for the actual year it was held, let alone who Mr and Mrs were.

I remember my first one very vividly. I was ten years old and had just been announced as head choir boy for the local village church. This was a big deal for me. I had been working my way up the cassock ladder since the age of seven. I could hold a tune better than most, looked good with my baby blonde hair and would have made an excellent model in a Freemans catalogue, if they had a child choir section, that is. I do believe I got the top job on merit but I did get a rather helpful hand from my predecessor, Alan Greenfold, aged thirteen, who unfortunately dropped the cross, halfway down the aisle, during one Sunday morning service. I still remember the gasps and sniggers to this day. The gasps were from the congregation, of course. The sniggers were from us choir boys and girls, looking from behind, as poor Alan tripped and fell in a heap, the large heavy cross gliding like an archer's arrow, down the aisle, and landing rather loudly some six feet away from his 'holster'. He never recovered from the shame, poor lad. He was also not forgiven by the tough, but lovable, Reverend Digby. And so it was, that the said Vicar offered me the coveted post.

To say that this extra responsibility went to my head was an understatement. There were fourteen of us in the choir. Four girls and ten boys. Apart from the Sunday morning service we attended in full cassock, we would rehearse once a week on a Tuesday and have a sort of mini-Youth club in the village hall on a Thursday. It was here we would play the usual daft children's games, and from my recollection, we did play 'Spin the Bottle' an awful lot. Is that even allowed now as a ten-year-old? It was whilst playing this particular game that I sampled my first kiss with a girl. Her name was Katy Redd. She was slightly older than me, at the grand old age of twelve, and had a lovely gentle persona with the aura of someone who would also kick the shit out of you if you crossed her.

I cannot quite remember the context, but I do remember spinning the bottle, it stopping, as it pointed at Katy, and me racing across the village hall to plant a rather awkward kiss on her lips. I thought I would be back on my bench seat within seconds but she held the kiss a tad longer than I had anticipated, me in a rather awkward position on my knees as she stayed glued to my mouth. I won't lie to you; I didn't know what to do or how to respond. Village life in the seventies didn't lend itself to learning the art of kissing. It did make me wonder how Katy had got so streetwise, that's for sure.

Apologies, I got a bit side-tracked and whimsical for a second. Back to the power-mad, ten-year-old head choir boy. I would use this authority to show I was in charge even when not required. I would keep the choir back at the end of rehearsal, citing that I wasn't happy with a particular hymn, when in reality I couldn't have given a toss and would rather have been playing Tin Can Alley in one of the farmers' yards. I just wanted to show them who was in charge. Maybe Katy thought I was more mature and confident than I actually was, hence the long kiss, but believe me, I wasn't. I just winged it and strutted about, oblivious to the resentment that was building up amongst our group.

And so it was, that my first wedding coincided with me having the honour of holding the newly damaged cross. You couldn't see the destruction if you held it a certain way but, in essence, the gold cross at the top had a large round dent that looked rather similar to the comedian Ted Robbins' chin. As long as said chin was pointed in my direction nobody would see what had happened.

The wedding was of a local couple from the village. Farmers. They had the monopoly when it came to utilising the church for nuptials, but then that's where the majority of children came from. I include the lovely Katy in this group. I hadn't yet moved to the small town with the five pubs, so I was surrounded by cows, sheep, and farmers' kids, with a whiff of hay accompanying them wherever they went. Don't get me wrong, it was idyllic.

The day of this particular wedding was gorgeous. It was late August and extremely hot. The stunning backdrop to the church, on days like that, is hard to describe. Surrounded by the hills, the bright blue sky and accompanying sunshine make the village seem the only place on earth to be. We had arrived early for one quick run-through of hymns and I was my usual bombastic self, criticising individuals for their 'pitch' or 'harmony'. Ridiculous looking back, and I knew I was losing the dressing room but, for some unexplained reason, I ploughed on. A ten-year-old dictator. Vicar Digby didn't seem to mind and I think he had a sneaky admiration for my leadership.

As we stood backstage, a final check that the frills on our cassocks were crisp and pristine, the vicar took me through my final instructions as the new head choir boy. A reminder to walk slowly, not to forget which way round the cross must now be and finally, once the cross is placed in its holster by the church organ, not to forget to kneel and nod towards Christ before taking my seat. He was at pains to emphasise taking my time in all my movements and outlining the importance.

Katy approached me to wish me luck. I responded that her hair was a bit messy and needed tidying up. Can you believe that? She turned on her heels, returning shortly after, with a can of Coke in hand and a big beaming smile, asking for approval. I nodded silently. As she turned away, she knocked her hands together, by accident, and the fizzy drink landed on my shiny black shoes. I was livid. I desperately wanted to throw a childish tantrum but we were behind a curtain, with the guests arriving a few feet from where we were congregated, so for the first time in my young life I threw a mute one instead.

Katy was all apologetic, whispering of course, and told me to take my shoes off and she would quickly clean them. Off she went, returning in double quick time, with another beaming smile on her face. To be fair, she had done a cracking job and so it was we got in line, waited for the church organ to play us in, and started the short journey down the aisle. I couldn't have been prouder at that moment.

I slowly made my way down, head upwards, like something out of Trooping the Colour. I made it to the end of the church, placed the heavy cross in its rightful place with no hiccups, and walked back to the carpeted steps to kneel and nod. This was done facing a statue of Christ so the guests and congregation only got to see the back of me. As I kneeled and held the moment, I heard loud gasps, followed by a trickle of laughter. This quickly became louder and more sustained until it felt like the whole church was at a Ken Dodd gig.

Rather oddly, and for no reason at all, I started to laugh too. It was all very infectious, and I was an immature ten-year-old, so joining in felt normal. I had no idea what was going on, especially behind me, but not for one second did I think that this packed holy venue was laughing at me. I finally got up from my kneeling position as the chuckling subsided. I knew I needed to get into my seat as that was the cue for the bride to make her grand entrance. It was as I stood upright that I felt a large hand on my small shoulder. I turned round to face a young man in morning dress, possibly the groom or best man, smiling gently at me. He leant towards my ear and I got a faint whiff of hay.

"Hey little fella," he whispered. "I think you have something on the sole of your shoes. Might be best if you go and get them cleaned up."

He gently ruffled my beautiful blond hair and gestured with a nod to a lady sitting opposite. At this point, I was a very confused little boy. My eyes were darting everywhere, not understanding what had been said and what was happening. The lady now had hold of my hand and we were walking back down the aisle towards the changing rooms. I remember looking up at her, gripping her hand rather tightly. She glanced back with a warm but sympathetic smile as we disappeared from the main event and behind the curtain. I sat on one of the benches and slowly took my shoes off.

"Don't worry about it love," the kind lady said, as I undid my shoelaces. "We have all been part of pranks. It's a part of growing up. You will laugh about this when you are older."

I looked down at my shoes and gradually turned them over to see the soles for the first time. I just stared for a few seconds as the enormity of what had just happened sunk in. My left sole was the first one that got my attention. Written in bold white was just the one word. 'Fuck'. You will probably guess what the right shoe said. Yep, you are right. The word 'Off'.

"I have to go now," the lady suddenly said, as I continued to stare at my size 4s. "The opening music has started. Will you be alright?"

I looked up at her, trying desperately to hold back the tears. "Yes," I lied, "I will be okay, thank you."

She bent down, gently stroked my left cheek and then went through the curtain, and back to the ceremony. I sat, silently crying, my shoulders shuddering like a pneumatic drill. I realise, looking back, that that was the first time I had ever felt true loneliness.

As I heard the organ playing the introduction, and the hustle and bustle of the bride arriving, I was all alone, a laughing stock. Whilst I knew that there would be repercussions, post-ceremony, I knew there and then that I might not be head choir boy going forward, and that hurt more than the humiliation that had just occurred.

In hindsight, I deserved it. Today it would probably be stated that I was a bully in that environment. And that would be the right call. A condescending, critical, self-centred little shit who rightly got his comeuppance. Ironic that, instead of battering me behind the bike sheds, Katy Redd used a far more subtle way to put me in my place. I have a sneaking admiration for her now and sometimes ponder where she is these days and what career path she followed. I think she will be doing just fine.

My first wedding, therefore, was a very memorable occasion and has stuck with me all my life. I learnt a huge amount about myself, even at such a tender age. I have been a leader since, in many vocations, and it's a good job I learnt how to take people with me all those years ago. Heaven knows how I would have turned out otherwise.

I also check my shoes regularly. The soles I mean. Habit, I'm afraid. One day I will get married and I will probably put them on the moment I wake up, even in the shower, just in case.

Chapter Two:

The year is 2012. I know what you are thinking. Hang on a minute, where did the last decade go? The last time we were following your incredible (!) tale, you had just become a father. Twice. I know. I apologise but I can't dictate our individual timelines. They are what they are and as this tale is about a hapless wedding, mine just happened to be in 2012. I was forty-two years old, bald, a tad overweight, with a dodgy back.

I had a wonderful, sensitive, ten-year-old daughter who I adored and spent as much time with as possible, in tandem with a twenty-three-year-old son who I didn't. More about that later. Finally, there was Dawn. You will be relieved to know that we were still together and that she would be the beautiful bride in this saga.

Back in 2001, after Charlotte was born, you may remember that I had been thinking of asking Dawn to marry me. That I was going to be decisive. Well, up to the beginning of 2012 I was still thinking, and as such been very indecisive. I don't know why it took me just over ten years to get down on one knee and ask for her hand. That didn't happen either to be honest. In the end, the never-to-be-forgotten proposal took place in our local Debenhams, one Saturday afternoon.

It was a bit of a ritual that every third Saturday in the month we would head into town for a 'sniff and snoop', as we called window shopping. I was bored rigid as Dawn and Charlotte meandered slowly through the concessions. I was swinging my keys on my forefinger and as we passed the make-up department, they suddenly flew off my farmer-sized digit, landing on a nearby counter, scattering keys and rings everywhere. Huge embarrassment ensued as I crawled on my hands and knees, in tandem with a customer adviser behind her station, desperately trying to locate these vital possessions.

Following much scrabbling around, we both dusted ourselves down and I carefully counted the keys to ensure all was in order. I then attempted to put them back in their rightful place on my keyrings. Why, in God's name, is it such a challenge to achieve a big enough gap to squeeze a key onto a ring without tearing a bloody fingernail off? After much muttering, with one or two male claws laying proudly on the counter, the challenge was completed although, like a lonely sock in a drawer, a spare ring was just lying there with no home.

Dawn had heard the commotion and was now by my side, her expression one of pity as she looked at me. What followed was pure, raw romance. In my head anyway.

"Hold out your left hand please," I said, in a matter-of-fact way. Dawn looked at me quizzically but complied.

"Not palm up," I said exasperated, as if she should know which way I desired. Dawn turned her hand over.

"Do you want me to close my eyes too?" she asked sarcastically. "I know you are bored, but can we do your Paul Daniels' impression when we get home?"

I ignored her jibe as I picked up the cheap plastic ring, black in colour, all chipped and faded. I stretched the wire slightly, took hold of Dawn's hand, and gently pushed this ridiculous, cheap item onto her finger. Dawn was staring.

Not at me, but over my shoulder at the assistant who must have been watching developments, probably with her mouth open like a guppy fish at feeding time.

"There you go," I said triumphantly. "You always say I am not spontaneous. Well, you can't get more spontaneous than this."

Charlotte was standing next to her mum, with a confused expression on her face. As for Dawn, let's just say I would probably have got a better reception from the Debenhams' assistant who, in all honesty, looked a bit giddy with the whole scenario. I looked at Dawn and she gazed back, for what seemed like hours. I still had hold of her hand with my symbol of commitment proudly in place for no one to see. She gently pulled her hand away and thrust it forward like she was mimicking an admiring look. She wiggled her fingers and the look wouldn't have been out of place in a Beaverbrooks.

"You're such a knob," she said, as she took hold of Charlotte's hand and meandered away in the direction of the shoe department.

"She didn't take it off though, did she?" I said, turning to the assistant who was now leaning on the counter, mesmerised by this sudden outpouring of romance.

"No, she didn't," she replied, standing up straight, suddenly remembering where she was. "But, and don't take this the wrong way, she is right. You are a bit of a knob." And with that, she turned around and walked to the other side of the counter where a lady was waiting patiently. "Yes, madam. How can I help?" she asked kindly.

I stood there for a few seconds and contemplated. They were both right, of course, but I had no regrets. In years to come, the two of us would remember this special moment and laugh at the absurdity of what had occurred and the uniqueness of my proposal. Is that not better than the traditional down-on-one-knee, in the most expensive restaurant in town, with yours truly giving a prepared speech? No? Must be just me then.

When I finally caught up with them both, ironically at the edge of the wedding department, it was as though nothing had happened. We carried on walking together, 'sniffing and snooping' until we made the mutual decision to abandon our excursion and go home. We had a takeaway. We watched The X Factor, with Dawn cooing over Gary Barlow and Charlotte constantly saying she wanted to be like Nicole Scherzinger when she grew up. Still, nothing was said but there was a strange, relaxed atmosphere and a general feeling that the deed had been done.

It is important to note that Dawn continued to wear the battered keyring on her finger and periodically I caught her, out of the corner of my eye, touching and twiddling it round and round. Thank God she has never been materialistic, I thought to myself, as I polished off the remains of a giant box of Maltesers, with the three of us sitting, all cuddled up on the sofa, as we patiently waited for Casualty to start. The two of them loved this TV drama, so I let them concentrate on Charlie and Co. as my thoughts turned to the wedding. *When*, of course, *Where* would be important, and finally *Who* we wanted there. There would be many discussions and decisions to be made but whatever happens, we would not, I repeat NOT, have an overflow evening reception for those waifs and strays who didn't quite make the cut for the main event.

Chapter Three:

The following morning, as I finished my shower and pulled back the curtain, I nearly jumped out of my skin as Dawn stood in front of me, head to one side, with a quizzical expression on her face.

"Have you any thoughts or ideas?" she asked.

"What about?" I answered, as I stepped out and put a large crusty towel around my ever-expanding waist.

"Sometimes you don't half say the wrong thing." she said, with a tinge of tiredness in her voice. "Take a wild guess."

"Ah," I replied, suddenly realising what she meant. "No. Not yet anyway. You?"

"Actually, I have."

Dawn was now sitting on the toilet, twiddling her 'money-couldn't-buy keyring' which was still in place on her finger.

"I would like to do it abroad, if possible."

Who said romance was dead?

There we were, cramped in the bathroom, with the post-department store, non-proposal, engagement keyring hanging off her finger, with a groom who had forgotten, and finally, back to the bride announcing she would like to 'do it abroad'. Even at that early stage, you got the feeling it was not going to be planned to the scale and intricacy of the Brink's-Mat robbery, that was for sure.

Getting married in a foreign land would, under normal circumstances, have filled me with horror, but we had been lucky enough to attend a wedding in Spain a couple of years before, so Dawn's request didn't bring me out in a cold sweat.

I was the best man for that particular shindig. The groom in question was called Kevin and he had been one of my friends from school. The bride was a Spanish lady, called Maya, that Kev had met on one of his frequent trips to that high-class resort, Fuengirola. Whilst the trip, ceremony, and reception didn't go as smoothly as any of us would have wanted, it will always live long in the memory.

We had agreed, as a family, to fly out two weeks before the Big Day. This was so that I was available if called upon, to assist with any errands required. I did what anyone with half a brain wouldn't do, and that was book a villa in the middle of nowhere. Far away from the church and reception, and, even worse, miles away from where Kevin was residing and counting on me for support.

The villa was privately owned and the couple who owned it, Wally and Denise, rented it out whilst living in a caravan down the hill, in a nearby field. Strange set-up in a way, but I suppose they made good money whilst living the simple life.

The good news was that I had hired a car. The bad news was that I had never driven on the right-hand side of the road.

I don't do stress, but I will make an exception with regards to driving abroad. To be honest, I wasn't worried beforehand. It just hit me when I set off from the airport, with Dawn navigating and an excitable Charlotte in the back. The concentration required, to follow signs and drive in the right direction, was draining. So much so that, on finally arriving at our villa, I spent the late afternoon and evening lying in bed with the mother of all migraines. In the morning, when Dawn suggested we ventured out to purchase some provisions, it did cross my mind to bury her alive, with the assistance of Wally, in the nearby field.

I dreaded the calls from Kevin. I need you in Malaga for this. Can you come over and help me with that? Twice a day in some instances. Each time, I would plonk my weary and stressed body into the car and go through purgatory, returning only to stumble straight into bed, head pounding. I never saw our private pool, let alone have a splash in it. Thankfully, the excursions came to a halt following a barbeque we attended, that was hosted by Maya's extended family, at a farm a few miles from our residency.

I don't eat fish. When I say fish, what I really mean is seafood. I am partial to the fish wrapped in newspaper and no harm is done by the battered or breadcrumbed type that lives in the freezer, but I have to decline politely when offered the likes of prawns, crab or lobster. Fundamentally, my tummy doesn't like them and, as such, makes the decision, rather quickly, to get rid.

So it was, as the barbeque was in full swing, I noticed that there was no meat. Anywhere. There were fish galore, sizzling away, with their eyes staring at you as though they were pleading for an escape route. More, prepped on large plates, seemed to be vying for space with the copious number of flies that had probably spread the word about this unexpected feast.

I should have just eaten the breadsticks and cheese, and saved myself for a drive-through McDonalds on the way home. But I didn't. Politeness took over, as did the overwhelming feeling that I needed to embrace their traditions and home. Their friendliness and generosity consumed you so much that you just wanted to please them. Be part of the family. So, I ate some prawns. Then some lobster. I spent a few minutes praying that my body would decide, in that instance, to let the food pass normally and be sympathetic to my situation and surroundings. Fat chance.

It started with the sweating. Then the stomach gurgling and cramps. Dawn had been in deep conversation with Maya's grandparents, hand gestures galore, so had not noticed me gorging on our sea friends. She would have stopped me. I walked over to her, with a weird feeling that I was floating like Tom Hanks in Apollo 13.

"Sorry to interrupt," I said urgently, "but I just need a quick word with Dawn."

I am sure that those ageing relatives hadn't a clue what I said but they nodded, smiled, and continued to nibble on a pile of pistachio nuts in front of them.

"Christ, you are dripping wet," Dawn stated, as she looked at my white T-shirt, damp with sweat. "You okay?"

"Not really. I have eaten some fish."

"You what? Why have you done that?" She suddenly looked anxious.

"How long?" she asked, knowing from experience the timescale from consumption to relinquish.

"Half an hour or so."

We both knew that we had approximately thirty minutes before I would be sick. Very sick.

Dawn decided that we needed to get back to the villa. I couldn't drive which was a plus given my stress issues, so she quickly found Kevin who in turn found his brother, Al, and before long we were on the road, colour draining from me by the second.

Poor Al. Maybe we should have been a bit more honest with him than the vague comment that I probably had a touch of sunstroke. The potholes and winding roads didn't help, and by the time we had reached our villa, the front passenger window, centre console, and 5-inch touch screen on the dashboard needed a rather deep valet.

To be fair to Al, he never once took his hands off the steering wheel or eyes off the traffic in front of him.

I think he did open his window though.

Chapter Four:

The wedding was four days away and I was bedridden. Not that it was important at that juncture, but we had been situated in our villa for eight days and I still hadn't sampled the pool. Thankfully, Charlotte got used to entertaining herself with her array of diving torpedoes. Usually, my seafood battle lasts about 24 hours but, for some reason, that deadline came and went, and I was still as sick as the proverbial dog. After 48 hours it was panic station time. I had just one day left to make a miraculous recovery and take up my duties as Best Man.

Dawn took the bull by the horns and made a call to the local doctor's number that was in our welcome pack. Let's be honest. Have you ever, on arrival at a holiday home, ensured you had a handle on the nearest hospital or surgery? Me neither. I wouldn't have known where to look, to be honest. Thankfully, Dawn was better prepared.

"The doctor is coming at about 6 pm," Dawn announced, as she picked up the glass of water by the bedside table and made me sip a little.

"Thanks," I whimpered. "What's he going to do?"

"No idea. I told him you haven't eaten for two days, that you are still being sick from both ends and that you have a wedding to get to tomorrow."

"Can't see him being able to help in time. Thanks, though."

The doctor was late and arrived at about 7 pm. He was a huge chap, rugby type, with a crusty beard. His English was perfect, making me feel ashamed for the umpteenth time with regards to my ignorance. He asked me a few questions and before I knew it, he was fumbling in his bag and produced the biggest needle I had seen since my grandma knitted me a sweater in the early 1970s. I sat up in bed and rubbed my arms, wondering which one he wanted. I don't like needles but if I close my eyes and sing any Take That song, out loud, I can get through it without too much mental anguish.

The doctor looked at me quizzically. "I'm sorry," he said, in a beautiful crisp accent, "I need you to kneel on your hands and legs, please. We are going through the bottom."

Now, I know what he meant, before anyone gets carried away with any sleazy thoughts. Though the realisation that he was going to whack that harpoon into my cheek filled me with total terror. I will need the whole of Take That's greatest hits, I thought to myself, as I got into position and lowered my shorts.

Is it not customary to give a warning before the deed is done? This doc didn't. One minute I felt him gently wiping the spot he has decided upon, and then; Christ Almighty. I'm not sure it was the shock of not knowing it was on its way, or it really was that painful and deep, but the scream that came out of my mouth would have woken Wally and Denise. Gary, Robbie and Co. didn't get a look in. I lay flat on my front, moaning, as Dawn settled up with the doctor. From my recollection, the knitting needle cost two hundred euros. I could make a joke about it being cheaper if I had had some sadomasochism, but I won't. I then fell asleep.

I woke bright and early. It was wedding eve. I gingerly started to get out of bed, fully expecting to still feel the nausea of the past three days. Nothing. I felt great. Knackered yes, but otherwise absolutely fine. It was a blessed miracle and I still have no idea, to this day, what the doctor syringed into me that evening.

The only plus from being ill for 72 hours, where nothing is entering the body but exiting at an alarming rate, is the weight loss. Now, in normal times, I would have been delighted to have shed a stone or two, but I had a morning suit hanging in the wardrobe which had been measured to the inch of its life to fit me.

I tried the whole outfit on. Let's not beat around the bush, I looked like a bloody clown. If you can try and picture it, yours truly was standing in a white baggy wing-collared shirt, with trousers and braces that were so loose I could have hidden a small baboon in them. My jacket hung off me like it was a 1980s shoulder pad tribute to Don Johnson. There was only one thing I could do, and that was to make an emergency visit to Malaga to get a quick refit, even though this would give me another migraine on my return.

Dawn had been sat on the bed during my fashion show and I knew for a fact she was stifling laughter as each layer went on. I let it ride, mostly due to fatigue.

"I will have to nip down to Malaga," I said, as I stepped out of the whole outfit without moving a muscle.

"You can't," Dawn replied. "The doctor said no driving for 72 hours, so you will be okay for the airport and going home, but not before."

Now I'm unsure whether Dawn had forgotten deliberately or that the previous few days had fuzzed her memory, but one of the reasons I hired a car in the first place was to be a wedding 'taxi' for the Spanish half of the family, from the church to the reception. At that point, what I should have done was ring Kev, tell him the situation, so he could find an alternative. But I didn't. Instead, I had a light bulb moment and decided to visit Wally and Denise at their caravan.

In the rare respites from my migraines and head down the toilet, I had met Wally and Denise a couple of times, early morning, whilst they were overlooking the field and their residency. It started with the obligatory waves to each other from afar and moved on to brief chats over the fence. They were a lovely couple. Elderly, but very active; especially Wally, who I watched chopping logs or polishing his beloved Mercedes. From what I could gather, they never went anywhere, saw anyone and were content just to live frugally, pocket the rental money, and occasionally pack up and have a few days away in their battered old camper van. It was the Mercedes I was interested in.

I opened the gate that led to their caravan and small land area. Wally was feeding the chickens, scattering food in all directions. He was dressed in baggy shorts and a hat that made him look like an elderly Crocodile Dundee. He looked up as I headed towards him.

"Morning," he said, in his lovely clipped southern accent. "Going to get up to 35 degrees today, so get creamed up."

"Morning. Thanks for the heads up," I replied. "Be good to try and get a bit of a tan before I go home."

"How's the wedding preparations going," Wally continued, still scattering the feed. "All ready to do your duties?"

"I think so, although the suit is a bit loose now. Won't bore you with the details. Let's just say the fish didn't agree with me. I do have a slight issue though and wondered if you could help."

Wally put the heavy sack down and made his way to a wooden seat that overlooked the beautiful hills. He removed his hat, wiped his forehead, and let out a tired sigh.

"I will try." He stood up, stretching his back. "What do you need?"

"Are you free tomorrow?"

I paused, and then just blurted out what I needed. "If so, I could do with your help as a driver, to ferry family and guests from the church to the reception. I can't drive at the moment and you wouldn't be insured for my car, so I was just hoping you would like a bit of a change and have a day out."

I paused again.

"You can join us for the reception if you like, as a thank you."

Why that last sentence came out of my mouth I will never know. Too late though. The offer was out there.

A huge beam spread across Wally's face. "I would be honoured to help out. I am sure I still have a suit somewhere, and a tie. Oh my, I haven't done anything this exciting for years. Thank you. I will have to call Denise and tell her. She will be so jealous to miss this."

"That's a shame. Is she away for a while?"

"Just for a couple of days." Wally was still beaming from ear to ear. "She will be livid. We never have anything exciting happen to us. When do you need me?"

"If you could be at the villa for 10.30 am, that would be perfect. The ceremony is at 12 noon at Malaga Cathedral, so if it's okay with you, drop us off and then be on hand just after 1 pm to escort some of the family guests to the reception."

"Wow. The Cathedral. Beautiful place. That's all good with me. I had better get organised."

"Thanks, Wally. You're a lifesaver. Any questions just shout out over the fence. One of us will be chilling out."

Wally was away, walking with more purpose than I had seen previously. It wouldn't have been a surprise if he had skipped his way back to the caravan, such was his excitement. I made my way back to the villa, content that I had managed to avert a mini-crisis, and not had to burden Kev with any last-minute issues. I still had my Charlie Cairoli suit that needed addressing but I hoped that Dawn had come up with a cunning plan.

"No," Dawn said, lying on a sunbed by the pool. "Not thought of a plan I'm afraid, although you could just wear extra clothes under the suit. That might do."

"I can see you have given it some deep thought," I replied. "You are probably right though. Let's hope it's not a scorcher then."

Chapter Five:

That evening, I made the call to Kev explaining the situation. He was delighted with the Mercedes plan, not so with my admission that I had invited Wally to the reception. Thankfully, he agreed to sort it and would find him a place on some table or other, preferably out of the way, which was a bit harsh, to be honest, but I sort of understood. I had no idea what attire he would find in the caravan, so caution was prudent in that scenario.

Strangely enough, I slept like a baby. I had worried that I would be going over my best man's speech, subconsciously, but the previous few days had finally caught up with me. So as the morning sun glistened through at 6.30 am, I bounced out of bed, grabbed a coffee, and sat in the garden, contemplating what was going to be a great day. I had, the evening before, had a dress rehearsal with regards to my 'clown' outfit. I wore the thickest pair of shorts I could find, and they worked okay with regards padding the trousers out, but the top half was a bit trickier and required two T-shirts (both white, phew!) to ensure that my wing-collared shirt and jacket fitted better, so dispensing with the 'Miami Vice' look. Dawn did remark that I then resembled 'Michelin Man', but I refused to rise to her sarcastic bait.

The rest of the morning was bedlam. Dawn and Charlotte hogged the main bathroom, argued over how much make-up she could wear; Charlotte that is. But by 10.30 am, we were all ready for the day's events. I had gone into the back garden, with a glass of chilled wine in my hand, a bit early I know, when I heard the loud scream. And then my name.

Dawn rushed towards me, fascinator unmoved, gesticulating with her arms, pointing back towards the villa.

"Christ, Dawn. What's up?"

"You need to come quickly. Don't go out the front door though, just look through the window." She was both animated and giddy, as though a wonderful surprise was awaiting us.

I followed her back inside, Dawn with her arm through mine, dragging me towards what? I had no idea. I got to the window where Charlotte was already stood, staring out. I looked out, leaning my head on Charlotte's shoulder. Not sure why, I suppose so that nobody or nothing could see me peeking out. No wonder Dawn had screamed. Stood in front of me on the driveway was a battered old camper van, clean and polished I grant you, but still a horrible yellow and white Volkswagen.

Stood proudly, by the side of this monstrosity, was Wally. To be fair to him he had found a suit, but I then realised the extent to which he said he never went anywhere. He looked like Austin Powers. I wish I could share the picture I took of him but unfortunately you will have to do with a brief description. It was blue. It was velvet. The only thing missing was the white fluffy cravat. He wore a pencil-thin red tie instead, which spoilt the International Man of Mystery's full look. To make matters worse, he had a gaping smile which, and I am really trying not to be unkind, gave way to teeth that could have been taken straight out of Mike Myers' chops and into Wally's. As an aside, he was also wearing his croc hat.

What would you have done in that situation? Go outside and tell him to 'get the hell out of here' and call a taxi instead?

Tempting, but all I could see was his face. The happy, joyous expression radiating in front of me through the window. How could I tell him that it was not what I had expected and that I was sorry, but we would have to make alternative arrangements? That this day and experience, which had probably left him sleepless with anticipation, was not going to happen. The answer was I couldn't, and I didn't. Stood behind me was a chortling Dawn, make-up dribbling down her cheeks from the tears she was shedding. I pulled myself together and opened the front door.

"Hiya Wally. You brush up well. That is some suit. Where's your Mercedes?"

Of course, what I desperately wanted to say was, "Where the hell is the bloody Mercedes, you cheap Austin Powers lookalike, with your rotten teeth and stupid hat?"

But, by then, I had resigned myself to not letting Wally down. I know what you are thinking. What a lovely gesture. Half true, the other half being that I don't like, or do, confrontation.

"Thanks," he replied, "I had to give it a brush down yesterday, so hopefully I won't embarrass anyone."

Hmmm. Not sure about that.

"The Mercedes? Denise has it. It's not a problem, is it? I promise you the camper is spotless, and it has leather."

And there you have it. Yours truly had completely left the detail out, far away in a distant galaxy. I had not noticed that the Mercedes was not by the caravan. I had not made it clear it was that car I required. In fact, I hadn't mentioned it at all. Just presumed. Well, you would, wouldn't you?

"No, it's fine," I lied. "Just would have been nice, that's all. The camper is fine. Anything to help us out."

Wally grinned again, but all I could think of was the faces of the happy couple when we rolled up looking like a lost family from the travelling community.

The journey down to Malaga was a bumpy one. It's a challenge through the tight, badly managed roads at the best of times. In a 1970's tin can? Not good. Charlotte was mortified, letting it be known that she didn't want to be seen dead in that contraption. At the grand old age of eight, she had discovered street cred and that was not it. Dawn on the other hand was having the journey of her life. She loved it.

There are many things I love about her and one is her self-depreciation. There she was, all dressed up to the nines, high heels, fascinator, new dress, and she was howling with laughter the whole journey. I can think of a few ex-girlfriends who wouldn't have taken the same view. One of them would have probably beaten Wally to an inch of his life.

Thankfully, nobody saw us arrive at the church. We were early, of course, as I needed to be with Kev and his posse of ushers for a debrief. The temperature had hit 30 degrees, it was mid-morning, and I was already beginning to sweat like a nun in a field full of cucumbers. Dawn and Charlotte stayed outside whilst Wally waved enthusiastically as he drove away, no doubt counting the minutes when he could return and be the attentive chauffeur. Christ Almighty, what a mess.

I didn't tell Kev, as he had better things to worry about. We stood at the front of the church as the guests started to arrive.

One of the ushers, Dan, came scooting down in a state of panic.

"Kev," he whispered, quite loudly, "we are trying to funnel the guests into bride or groom sides but they are all ignoring us and sitting anywhere."

"Don't worry about it," replied Kev. "It will be fine. Just let them sit where they want."

"I will come and have a look, Dan," I said, seeing the worried expression on his face. "Won't be long, Kev."

We purposely walked to the back of the church where the remaining ushers were trying to hand out service booklets, but no one was taking up the offer. Similar to when you are handing out double glazing leaflets I imagine. The volume of guests was also increasing at a rapid rate and was beginning to overwhelm the 'doorkeepers.'

"Guys, I would let it go. Leave them to just come in and find a seat. I don't think you can call on a rescue team to help if you get trampled on by the incoming stampede."

I ushered them away, stood back and watched open-mouthed at what was unfolding.

It didn't take me long to realise what was happening. We stiff upper lip Brits have a protocol at a wedding. Guests invited. Guests arrive. We usher them to their seats depending on whether they are there for the bride or groom. All very structured and traditional. Not here. Not in Spain. It was principally a free-for-all. There were guests, of course, and you could tell them by their attire, but alongside were everything from shopkeepers and butchers to tourist backpackers and even the homeless. Trust me, there were hundreds of them. By the time I had scarpered back to the safety of Kev, it was standing room only. I could only hope that Dawn and Charlotte had managed to get in. It crossed my mind to try and find them, but it would have been like looking for a piece of hay in a stack full of needles. I sat down, patted Kev on his shoulder and got into best man character.

The ceremony was beautiful. It was grand, romantic and spiritual. You actually felt the love and warmth in that vast religious site. When a hymn was sung, the acoustics bounced off the walls. It gave you goose pimples. You won't be surprised to learn that the harmonies that came out of the local butchers' and fishmongers' mouths put the three tenors to shame. I should have guessed in all honesty.

As we walked back down the aisle, deed done, my immediate thoughts turned to how this joyous moment was about to be ruined by the sight of Austin Powers and his Scooby-Doo van.

I managed to track down Dawn and Charlotte, who thankfully had survived the earlier stampede and were in one piece. We walked out into the sunshine, the three of us holding hands, definitely the calm before the storm.

Chapter Six:

"Where's your man and his Mercedes?"

Kev had sidled up to us.

"I can't see him in the loading bays. Nani and Tata are ready to go."

The grandmas. Time to come clean.

"Sorry Kev, I couldn't get the Merc in the end and didn't want to bother you."

The radiant bride Maya had now come to join Kev. This could get messy.

"He is here. In fact, if you look, he is waving frantically at us."

Kev and Maya looked down the expansive church steps, scouring the area where a couple of cars were in situ ready to chauffer the VIPs to the reception. Their head movements stopped when they spotted a man gesturing at us.

"Is that him?" asked Kev. "The one who looks like bloody Johnny English?"

"I think you mean Austin Powers, but yes, that's him. He was a bit short of suit choice."

"Not bothered which secret agent he is aspiring to be if I'm honest. Where's his car?" Kev was getting a bit exasperated by this point. Totally understandable.

"He is standing next to it. You can't miss it." And you couldn't, unless you were Stevie Wonder.

"You are kidding? He's got a camper van?"

He was shouting now and to be honest I couldn't think of anything to say. Maya had started to cry, and Dawn was trying to console her with words of how much fun it had been travelling down in it. Not sure that was helping.

Before we could discuss further, Wally had bounded up the steps, still grinning, and was now amongst us. I feared for his life at this point, so I took a step back, being the proverbial coward, and let Wally take the flack. He introduced himself to Kev and then sidled over to Maya, still tearful, and proceeded to have, what I can only describe as, a robust conversation. In Spanish. It hadn't crossed my mind that Wally could speak fluent Spanish, which is a tad ignorant when the bloke had been living in Spain for decades. He was very good, and I found myself drawn to listening to his every word even though I hadn't a clue what he was saying.

And then Maya laughed.

Wally gave her a kiss on both cheeks and then disappeared into the throng of guests, reappearing with the grandparents, guiding them down the steps, and towards his camper van. As they approached the vehicle, I noticed some of the guests, plus one or two of the local tradespeople, had followed them down. I could hear lots of laughter and my curiosity got the better of me, so I joined the small group to see what all the fuss was about. The scene on arrival was, to put it mildly, surreal.

Basically, Wally, the grandparents, and the trusty old camper van had become one giant photo opportunity and his wheels a weird attraction. There were poses inside, leaning on the side, sat in the driver's seat, all whilst cameras were flashing as Wally held court. At one point I thought we were missing a trick and could have charged for this privilege. The grandparents were laughing loudly, soaking in the attention. After what seemed like an hour, they boarded the tin can and, on departure, waved enthusiastically, with huge smiles, as we all waved back. I'm not sure what I had just witnessed but it was a blessed relief compared to what could have happened.

The reception venue was only a ten-minute round trip so Wally kept returning, guests lined up by the side of the road, jostling to be the next recipients of this attraction. Wally was in his element, a magnificent chauffeur host in his velvet attire. It truly was a sight to behold. I stood and watched in awe for a while, looking at the smiling faces all desperately trying to have their photo taken. He caught my eye and just winked.

The reception went without a hitch and my speech went down a storm. Well, with the British contingent that is. The Spanish side sat and listened in stony silence. Not because they didn't think it was funny, or that I was being rude, just that they had no bloody idea what I was saying. I managed to catch up with Wally later in the evening, who in the end had bagged himself a place on a table near the front, to the delight of most of the guests. He was a huge hit all day.

"What on earth did you say to Maya to stop her crying?" I asked him, as we stood by the bar.

"I just said that what I had brought was unique. That weddings can all just merge into one if not careful. That my camper and I would give a once-in-a-lifetime memory for her and her family. One that they will talk about for many years. I just said, trust me. I am an honorary Spaniard so would never embarrass her or her nationality. Then she laughed, so everything was okay."

He was still smiling, and I just shook my head.

"Thank you," he continued, "I have had the best day ever. I rang Denise earlier and she had to calm me down I was babbling away so much. She is gutted to miss all of this."

I shook his hand, followed by a manly bear hug. He turned back to the bar and ordered a treble Jack Daniels and Coke.

"Steady Wally, I know you are leaving your camper here for the night, but the evening is still young."

"I know, but I have no idea what time they are shutting the free bar, so got to get it whilst the going is good."

Normally I would baulk at such greed, but I didn't begrudge him a bucket load of JDs. He'd earned each and every shot.

I don't remember all of the evening that followed. We did push on until the sun began to rise, which was a feat in itself, following the carnage of the days leading up to it. Dawn mentioned, a tad late in the proceedings, that the doctor had also advised that I shouldn't drink. I have a feeling she kept that important announcement to herself so as not to spoil my day, God love her.

Back in our villa the following day, we nursed our hangovers and chilled in the back garden. Occasionally, I spotted Wally pottering on his land and we would give each other a wave from afar. I thought about going over, to see if he was okay, but in all honesty, I was exhausted and found it difficult to have a meaningful conversation with Dawn and Charlotte, let alone anyone else.

Before we knew it, our time was up and we were heading home. We never went back. Never saw Wally again. We contemplated returning, but we kept coming back to the conclusion that the special memory we had acquired should stay that way. When we look back, flicking through the photos and reminiscing, we never talk about my migraines or acute diarrhoea, we just talk about Wally. And laugh very much.

Chapter Seven:

It is often forgotten that the bridegroom has many things to think about and organise once an engagement is official. There are the morning suits to choose. A best man. And that's about it. We chaps pretend we are involved with everything else, but the reality is your bride to be, the parents of said bride, and the best friend of your beloved are in control of events. There were many things to consider, plus the added complexity of the wedding being held abroad. Destination unknown.

That was all fine by me, as I needed time and space to make the right decision with regards to my wingman for the big day. I had a huge choice. Actually, that is not true, but I thought it was when I sat down to write my list of candidates. The reality was a pick of four. My elder brother, Craig, my best friend from primary school, Phil, Spanish Kev, or a good friend from my late teenage years, Big Mac. I know what you are thinking. Big Mac must have loved a visit to a certain burger giant. Unfortunately not. Up in the Yorkshire Dales, we didn't even have a bloody supermarket, let alone a fast-food drive-through. His nickname came about because he was, how do I put it? Huge. At six foot seven and over twenty stone, he was a man-mountain, but a lovable summit.

I soon discounted Phil. I hadn't spoken to, or seen him, for over fifteen years, so he would have found it a bit odd to be asked to be Best Man to someone he didn't know anymore, to a woman he had never met. Craig was the obvious choice but, although I loved him very much, I was wary of him not being able to get out of police-mode and end up vetting the guests, having sniffer dogs at the venue, and searching bags on arrival at the church. He just can't help himself.

Spanish Kev would have been a nice reciprocal choice, but we had lost touch since his wedding, and he was firmly planted in Spain which would make it hard for the forthcoming arrangements. That left Big Mac, and whilst he could at times be overpowering with his booming voice and presence, he was a great guy. The life and soul of any party. I knew he would have my back for the duration of whatever we ended up planning. I also knew he would feel honoured to be asked.

I first met him when I joined a bunch of lads that formed the core of the 'Famous Five' pub crawls. Craig had persuaded me to tag along, reminding me that I had turned eighteen and, as such, needed to 'learn the ropes'. It was pretty obvious that Big Mac was the leader of the group and was like a Marlon Brando, Godfather figure. At the time, I was semi-single as although I was occasionally seeing Louise in London, I couldn't see a long-time future in it even though the bright lights dazzled me on each visit. It was Big Mac who would always ask after her when I returned. He would genuinely enquire what we had been up to, how I should think about taking the relationship more seriously, moving down there, and getting out of the shit show. If there was anyone I could, and should, have told about what happened on my final visit to Lou, then he would have been that man. He would have given sound advice too. I wish I had now.

He knew how to drink and what his limit was. He boasted that he could drink nine pints of bitter and still pass a breathalyser test. How can you ever prove something like that? He did, one evening, with yours truly in the back of his battered old Hillman Hunter. We were travelling back from one of those pubs situated in the middle of nowhere. I had certainly had seven drinks and missed a couple of rounds so I am pretty confident that the nine-pint threshold had been met that evening. I know we should have got a taxi, but we were in the Dales and they were in short supply, if not nearly non-existent. As the police flagged him down, his confidence never wavered. I think.

My brother Craig was in the front, his pre-police days, and was chuckling away whilst goading Big Mac to "tell them where to shove it." How times change. So, there we were, by the side of the road, with this huge hulk of a man standing on the pavement blowing his heart out into a bag. Personally, I thought we would be walking home but, after a few minutes, the officers thanked him for his cooperation and wished him well for his onward journey.

"Blimey," Craig said all excitedly. "That was awesome. Did you not worry just one teeny bit?"

"Of course, I did," he bellowed, in a voice that can only be described as being akin to Brian Blessed. "I shit myself, to be honest, but got away with it."

"You did say you could do nine pints," I said, in a far too congratulating way. "So fair play, Big Man."

"It was ten actually. I had one in The Fox whilst I was waiting for you two tossers to turn up."

And, with that, he roared with laughter as we hurtled down the back roads to home.

As I spent more time with Big Mac, so we got friendlier and enjoyed each other's company. He was four years older than me, and I did look up to him. That was probably okay through any daytime get-togethers, but not so good in the evenings. He worked at the local paper mill and his shifts meant that he had the odd days off through the week. It was similar to my hotel work and so we would sometimes go out for the day. On one of those occasions, he asked if I wanted to accompany him to Pontefract as he needed to pick up a wine-making device and, as I had bugger all to do, I joined him to keep him company.

The collection went without a hitch and we began our journey home. Not to bore you too much, but it entailed joining the A1, then taking the M62 to Manchester, off at the M1 heading to Leeds, through Leeds and then finally on the A660 to the Dales. These are important details to be aware of as events unfolded.

Joining the A1 does require a degree of concentration, as otherwise, you are likely to be wiped out by some articulated lorry or other. This particular time was different. We couldn't see any traffic in front of us as we ambled down the slip road. As we merged, we could see cars behind us, but they seemed to be in a line and going at a very steady pace. We soon realised why, as we drove towards what looked like a police van and behind it three BMW police cars. They were hogging the lanes, weaving in and out, I presume to ensure they were not going to get ambushed. Somehow, we had ended up being the first car behind this prisoner movement. They were certainly safe with us in Big Mac's Hillman Hunter, that was for sure.

My big buddy started to have a bit of personal fun, by going into the outside lane as though he was going to try and pass, only for one of the BMWs to come across and 'close the door', so to speak. He was chortling away, amusing himself, as we crawled up the dual carriageway.

"Hopefully, we can get going again when we come off and join the M62," I said, as Big Mac tried another pretend manoeuvre.

Our luck was out. The mini convoy came off at the junction, with little old us still behind them. Big Mac let out a frustrated grunt, but soon mellowed when we joined the three-lane carriageway and he decided to have a bit more fun, occasionally accelerating, weaving across lanes, watching them cover his every move.

"Don't piss them off too much, Big Man, the last thing we need is to get arrested."

"It's fine. They will know who I am. Done a plate check, I would have thought. They should be thanking me for keeping them alert. Good practice for them."

And so it continued. They came off to join the M1 to Leeds, as did we, Big Mac ensuring he joined right behind them again. We then finally left the motorway and headed through the city centre. The vehicles in front of the convoy parted like the Red Sea and we just kept on following, heading towards the A660 and home. We had been behind them for approximately thirty miles and well over an hour and a half in time.

As we approached the courthouse area (you are well ahead of me, aren't you?), the BMWs suddenly jammed all on and blocked the road in front of us.

"Hey up," said Big Mac, as he stopped the car. "Something has spooked them up ahead."

He was wrong. It was behind them.

What happened next was all rather surreal. Just a mass of armed police clambering out of the cars, shouting rather loudly. At us. Instructions to get out of the car, to get our hands up in the air. I felt a strange sense of panic, intimidation, but also exhilaration. It was an odd combination as I lay flat out on the road, with a gun pointing to the back of my head. I tried to remember being a ten-year-old choir boy again so that I could pray. I could hear Big Mac's muffled voice, so I was guessing he was trying to explain to an officer whilst his face was pressed against the tarmac.

After what seemed hours, we were back on our feet. I was shaking, and kept my mouth firmly shut as Big Mac stuttered his way through his explanation and before long, we were back in our trusty getaway Hillman Hunter.

"Why did they stop us?" I asked, as my heart rate finally returned to normal.

"I asked them the same thing," he said, as we meandered through the beautiful Yorkshire countryside. "They just said their suspicions grew as we kept following them."

"What did you say? I suppose they were partly right."

"I just said we wanted to get home. That I worked in a paper mill, we were just country bumkins, that even if we had been ready to ambush them and take the prisoner, would we honestly get very far in this bloody contraption? They said

I shouldn't have been weaving all over the place and accelerating towards them all the time."

He paused and smiled.

"My response was that it was the most excitement that had come along in years, and they would understand if they lived in a no man's land like us."

He laughed, in his usual Brian Blessed tone, but I could see that his hands were still slightly trembling, as he steered the car carefully around the tight bends, towards the safety of home.

You are probably thinking that he might not be the best choice for the best man. That he could be a bit of a liability, come the Big Day. I totally agree, but it didn't stop me from picking up the phone to ask him.

"Can't wait," he bellowed, on my request.

Oh well, I thought, whatever happens, it won't be a dull wedding, that's for sure.

Chapter Eight:

We had been lucky enough to holiday in one or two destinations as a family, so the decision was made to pick our favourite from the past ten years for our forthcoming nuptials. This was not as easy as it sounds as we had been fortunate enough to visit Spain, France, Tunisia, The Gambia, Italy, West Indies, Australia, and Edinburgh. I had included the last one as it took us the same time to get there, on a bloody train, as it did to the small West African country.

We made a list of all the areas that we had visited and somehow Charlotte had added California to it. I hazarded a wild guess that this was somehow linked to her desire to visit Disneyland, but as that destination didn't pass our initial test of countries visited, she was a bit goosed. Being the astute ten-year-old she had become though, she just crossed it out and highlighted Paris instead. This was a bit trickier to navigate. Yes, we had been to Paris, but no, we hadn't been to see Mickey Mouse. For the moment, it stayed on the list and I knew at least one vote had been cast already. It was a good job there were three of us.

I wanted the wedding in Barbados. Not for any other reason than because of Coughlin's Law. Does anyone remember that? At this point, I will make a little confession. Before I met Dawn and was in the rather toxic relationship with Susan, I had made some discrete enquiries with regards to leaving Blighty, and the blessed Yorkshire Dales, to become a barman in the Caribbean. I had the experience and I had watched the film Cocktail, in secret, of course. I wanted to be Tom Cruise behind that bar on the beach.

There were a couple of problems with that plan. Firstly, I didn't have the money to get there and, secondly, I was already bald and a tad podgy, even in my twenties. I don't think I had the look the owners of those relaxing cocktail bars were after, to be honest.

The bald situation was rather odd. When I was eighteen, on Christmas Eve, I wandered into our local barber and asked him to give me a number one all over. No idea why. Possibly my rebellious phase that lasted all of ten minutes. My mother was not impressed when I turned up for Christmas dinner looking like Phil Mitchell's long-lost son. The problem is, it never grew back. Not properly anyway, so, from my official end of childhood, I looked a bit daft.

I have digressed again. Barbados was soon ruled out on account of distance and cost for family and friends. Fair enough. Big Mac would probably have needed two plane seats, so the shorter the excursion the better, really. He had already rung me and suggested Germany. This wasn't on our list, but we had been in touch, and I had informed him we were looking at the month of October for the big day, so he needed to keep it free. No decision had been made at that point, I said, hence his intervention. He was very keen, talking about the culture and architecture and was very persuasive until I realised the real reason that he fancied that particular country. He wanted to devour the Munich Beer Festival, or Oktoberfest, as it is better known. Can you imagine the carnage? Would Munich actually have had enough beer for that glutton monster? I said no.

We contemplated Spain, but the memory of Kev's wedding and Wally's star turn were still fresh in the memory and we didn't want comparisons to be made. It had, however, given us a handle on logistics and travel with regards people, having had some involvement with organisation of that as his best man.

Australia was soon ruled out on account of being similar to the Caribbean with regards to a long-distance destination. Tunisia was still on the list, but Dawn soon scrubbed that out, on account of me spending two nights in the slammer whilst we were supposedly enjoying a week's break, in 2007.

It was a case of mistaken identity, to be honest. We had booked a babysitter, courtesy of Thomsons, so we could have an evening to ourselves. We had ventured out, had a nice meal, and decided to enter a local nightclub close to where we were staying for a bit of a dance. I had purchased a couple of drinks at the bar and, as I headed back to our table, I got nudged due to the volume of people in the club, dancing away. One of the drinks, a Ruby Red Breeze cocktail, toppled to my right and unfortunately landed all over a Tunisian chap's crisp white shirt.

I was trying to apologise as Kung Fu Fighting, by Carl Douglas, boomed out of the resident music system, which was rather apt as events began to unfold. He was shouting at me, in Arabic of course, when a man I had never seen in my life approached and stood behind me. Then, without warning, he launched his fist over my right shoulder and plonked this poor guy onto his backside. For the casual observer, it might have looked as though I was a physical freak. Two glasses, one in each hand, with a third hand, free to knock a guy spark out.

Bedlam. That is the only word I can use for the few minutes that followed. I was stood in the middle of the dance floor as the fists flew, chairs were launched and glasses were smashed. I never threw a punch and never got hit. It was like a scene out of The Naked Gun film where the carnage occurred all around Frank Drebin, as he shouted, "Nothing to see here." I was Frank.

It wasn't long before the Tunisian police landed to break the fight up, rounding up the protagonists like confetti. Yours truly became collateral damage. It was pointless trying to explain, in a posh Yorkshire accent, that you were innocent and not involved except for accidentally spilling a red drink on a perfectly pressed white shirt. Dawn's face, as I was led out into a waiting police van, was just pure shock and horror. That was one of those rare occasions where even she couldn't find a sarcastic angle, on which she thrived.

I have had better days if truth be told. The Dales could sometimes feel like a prison but at least you had the Three Peaks to look at. I just had graffiti-covered concrete walls, with what could only be described as a busted-sofa mattress. Our Thomson rep did a sterling job and, after a day and a half, I was released. The proviso though, was that I had to leave the island on the next available flight. I was quite happy to accept those terms, although Dawn and Charlotte took more persuading. We did have four days of our holiday left after all.

So it was, that our list was now left with France and Italy. The risk of Paris, and Charlotte's desire to shake hands with Donald Duck, made the decision easier.

"I always wanted Italy," Dawn admitted one morning, as she devoured a large bowl of Charlottes Frosties.

"That's good then," I replied. "Although are you sure? I mean, you did go through the mill a bit there."

"I was just unlucky. Just one of those things. I will be fine next time."

To be fair, we did have a lovely holiday there. Well, I did. Charlotte did too. The one who had a nightmare was poor Dawn. We had booked a little house, in the middle of nowhere, just outside Bari, in the southern area of Italy. It was idyllic, just outside a little non-tourist village. It was baking hot in the daytime and stifling at night, even with the fans working overtime.

It was following our first evening that Dawn's nightmare began. She woke up with a few bites. You will be familiar with them. Pesky midges, possibly the odd mosquito, but we were well-prepared and cream was applied, as per usual. The second morning she had more, and I mean, a lot more. Like a dot-to-dot book. Face, arms and legs covered with the little buggers. By the time she woke up on the fourth morning, you could hardly see any part of the skin that didn't have a bite. It was horrendous. For her anyway. We contemplated going home, such was the discomfort, but Dawn managed to find an antihistamine cream from a local pharmacy that worked miracles.

"You just need to be aware," I continued, ensuring that she remembered how she had felt at that time. "There is a slight risk you could get attacked again. It was okay last time as you could stay in bed and itch the living daylights out of yourself. This time you will be getting married, in front of family and friends. I have no desire for you to be mistaken for a braille board."

"Knob," she muttered, as she finished loading the dishwasher. "It was a one-off. Probably won't happen again. Our doctor said the same thing. We can take better precautions anyway. I want to get married in Italy, okay? Actually, what I really want, is to get married in Puglia. The Borgo Egnazia Hotel, please."

Dawn brushed past me, gave a little smile, and headed upstairs. I have no idea why we went through the charade of a list, as it was obvious that she had decided the destination and venue for our special day a long time ago. My guess is that she had already made her mind up when we were in the bathroom, that morning, having a general discussion.

I wished, right then, that I had had a female equivalent to her 'knob' jibe which she always aimed at me.

Chapter Nine:

Finding an appropriate date for a wedding is a minefield in itself. Traditionally, here in the UK, most couples tend to gravitate towards a summer wedding, praying for a scorching hot sunny day. Then there are those who love the feel of a Christmas wedding, still praying for a sunny day of course, but a crisp and freezing one instead. As we had chosen abroad, we didn't have this conundrum but if you had asked me which I would have chosen then it would have been Christmas all day long. It feels more magical to me, plus the fact that the summer dates you probably desire have all been booked up until 2052. You will have split up by the time it was your turn to say, "I do."

As you may recall, we had ringfenced a week in October. I can't remember why exactly, but I think it was to do with climate and availability for close family and friends. The dates we had set aside were Saturday 13th to Sunday 21st with the actual wedding pencilled in for 18th, 19th or 20th. This gave us flexibility before having to head home on the 21st and back to that dull thing called work.

Dawn had set her heart on the Borgo Egnazia Hotel in Puglia, Italy. A fine choice, I have to say. Apart from her body being a continuous meal for the local mozzies, we had had a wonderful holiday in that area, culminating in a fabulous lunch at that exquisite hotel.

What. A. Place.

Situated in the middle of nowhere, it was luxury personified. We vowed, as we drove back to our holiday house, that we must go back and stay at that gorgeous abode. This was our chance.

We did have a budget, but we also had a contingency kitty. This was courtesy of one of Dawn's uncles, who had passed away the year before, leaving quite a large wad to Dawn and his other nieces and nephews. This was, as normal with these surprises, to be kept for things we really wanted or needed. A new kitchen, for example, Charlotte's schooling maybe. Or a dream wedding. In the end, we decided the kitchen would have to wait, and Charlotte would have to go up a chimney and earn a living.

So it was, one Saturday morning, I got comfy in our desk chair, pad and pen at the ready, and made the call to ascertain availability and cost.

"Good morning, Borgo Egnazia Hotel. How can I help you?" the friendly, but professional, voice answered.

"Hi. Yes, hopefully, you can. We are looking to get married at your hotel so I am just enquiring with regards to dates and cost."

"I am sure we can help, Sir. Please bear with me and I will put you through to the Events Department. I am just transferring you now."

There was a pause as some beautiful operatic music played down the line. I took a sip of coffee as I waited patiently.

"Good morning, Sir." A new voice. Italian of course, young from the first impression. "My name is Angelo Romano. How can I help you this fine morning?"

"Hi Angelo," I started, trying to sound as affluent as possible so that I didn't hear the dialling tone before I got my request out. "We are looking to book your establishment for our wedding this October."

"Of course, Sir. What date were you requesting?"

"Preferably Friday 19th, if that is available."

"Please wait, Sir. I will just check." There was a brief silence. "I am sorry, Sir, but this date is already booked. Do you have any alternatives?"

"Well, we could do 18th or 20th, although that would be a bit tight with flights home the following day."

"Let me have a look, Sir. It looks like those days are booked too. I am sorry."

"Okay. Don't worry. It's not your fault. What about 14th, 15th, 16th or 17th. We are out there for all those dates too, so we could adjust our plans."

"I think those are booked too, Sir," the young man stuttered. "I am sorry."

"You think?" I said politely. "Would you mind double checking. Just in case one of the dates is free please."

"One moment, Sir."

I heard him put the phone down, followed by muffled talking. I could faintly hear the young chap, Angelo, querying the diary, that it was blocked out but with no names. I then heard a second voice, followed by snippets of some of the words that were plain and direct. 'Had to be kept clear - wedding 19th October - the whole week - Mr Timberlake.'

I stayed sat, slightly excited, waiting for Angelo to pick up his phone.

"I am so sorry, Sir. It looks like we have bookings for the whole week."

"That's a shame," I replied, guessing why the whole week was booked out, "but I suppose I can't compete with Justin Timberlake, so I will bow out gracefully."

"Please hold, Sir," Angelo suddenly sounded agitated. The phone went down again and a muffled, rather heated, discussion between the two men ensued. I waited patiently as I heard more words. 'Secret - offer something - free.'

Angelo returned once again.

"My manager has just advised that we can offer you a complimentary weekend here at the Borgo Egnazia, for you and your wife, at your leisure. But my manager has stated clearly that you must not mention Mr Timberlake's name to anyone, no dates, and no mention of a wedding. Would that be suitable for you?"

To be honest, it was very suitable, thank you very much. It wouldn't have crossed my mind to tell anyone that we couldn't get married in our desired venue because Justin Timberlake had beat us to it. Actually, that's not strictly true. I would have told Dawn, Charlotte, my brother Craig, Big Mac, both sets of families and anybody I bumped into who would enjoy the tale. They were right to buy me off in hindsight.

"Thank you, Angelo," I said. "I would be delighted to accept your kind offer. Mr Timberlake has made a fine choice for his wedding."

"Please, Sir. No names, if you please."

"Sorry. Won't mention him again. Promise."

"Thank you. If you can give me all your details, I will email you our offer alongside an NDA for you to sign and return if you please."

"Of course, Angelo," I said, as I gave him my details as quickly as possible in case his manager changed his mind.

Disappointed? Not at all. A bit of a relief, actually. I had done a few calculations whilst perusing their website and the wedding, if held there, would have wiped us out of our savings, including Uncle Brian's inheritance. Maybe if I had written and recorded 'Cry Me a River' we would have been in a better position.

I came off the phone and wandered into the back garden where Dawn was planting some early spring flowers.

"How did you get on?" she asked.

"Well, there is good and bad news."

"Go on," she said, continuing to dig away.

"The bad news is that the week we want is booked up so we need to find an alternative venue. The good news is that we have got a free weekend there whenever we want."

Dawn stood up and looked at me quizzically.

"Why on earth would they offer a free weekend, just because they are fully booked? It doesn't make sense."

"Ah well," I started, barely able to contain myself. "Justin Timberlake is getting married there that week and I wasn't supposed to know as it's a secret, but to cut a long story short I overheard, so they gave me a freebie to keep my mouth shut."

"Why do you make such shit up?" she exclaimed, her digging turning rather violent. "You can be such a knob sometimes. What's the real reason?"

I laughed.

"I know I do. Sometimes. But this one is bang on true. I have an NDA winging its way for me to sign. You can see it for yourself. I'm not supposed to tell ANYONE so, for God's sake, don't tell any of your friends. Or Charlotte for that matter. Even at the age of ten she is a bit savvy, and it would be all over the place in no time if we told her."

"Bloody hell," Dawn laughed, as she sat down. "Dream wedding ruined by Justin Timberlake. I can just see the headline. Could be worse reasons, I suppose. Well done for negotiating a freebie though. Did you play it tough? Like negotiating a sale?"

"Yep," I lied. "They didn't offer me anything at first, but I just said I couldn't be held responsible if it got out. Not my fault they were a bit lax in their conversations while I was supposedly on hold. Blah, blah. I went from coffee and biscuits to a whole weekend."

"Aw. Thank you. I will look forward to that very much."

She smiled. "Now go and hunt me a new wedding venue please."

She shook her head. "Justin Timberlake…!"

There is nothing wrong with a little white lie now and again. She didn't need to know that they had just plonked that fabulous offer in my lap. It made me look strong and a no-nonsense sort of chap for my bride-to-be. In reality, I would have whimpered a 'yes, of course' at a cup of tea in the staff kitchen.

We never did tell anyone. When anyone asked why we couldn't get our dream venue, we would mysteriously say we were unable to answer for security reasons. We enjoyed being interrogated for more information and not being able to elaborate any further. Everyone found out, of course, when it was plastered all over Hello Magazine at the end of October.

The pictures of Mr and Mrs Timberlake's wedding looked fabulous. We still have a few press cuttings of the happy couple which we cut out and stuck in a photo book. Sometimes we drag it out from the loft, have a look through, and pretend it is us in the photos.

Same date. Same area. Just them at our dream venue, instead of us.

Chapter Ten:

The dreaded guestlist. Normally this is a conundrum in any bride and groom's planning. That first day you both sit down and start the long tortuous process of who you want to invite, who you don't, and who you have to. The early stages are nice and easy. Close family, best friends and possibly your favourite work colleagues appear on the guest list within minutes. Then the arguments start. The groom's friend that the bride cannot abide, or vice versa. The embarrassing uncle or auntie that could spoil the whole day but, if not invited, could create a family rift of huge proportions that could last for years.

Thank God we were buggering off abroad then. We didn't have this problem. We could invite those that we really wanted to, whilst being able to use the excuse for the others that, as the wedding was overseas, numbers were limited. We had decided on a maximum of thirty to accompany us to Italy but put together names for fifty, just in case. We were well aware that some of our first choices may decline an invite due to cost or work commitments, even though we had sounded out the majority with regards to the wedding already and had received positive noises from most.

The one predicament I faced was that of my son, Peter. For those of you who may have forgotten, or slept since the first tale, here is a quick recap. Peter is my son that I didn't know existed for the first twelve years of his life. Born to my nurse girlfriend, Louise, who was the spitting image of Peter Beardsley and lived in London. She became pregnant, had our son, whilst I had scuttled back to the Dales, with the impression that she was having a termination and blocked the whole emotional experience out of my head.

The intervening years had not been as easy as TV soaps and dramas would have you believe. In their world, a long-lost child appears; there is some friction for a while, but within a few episodes everything is fine and dandy and they live happily ever after. Real life, as we are all too aware, is not that like. It can hurt us badly.

It was in 2001 when I first knew about Peter, just as Charlotte entered this world. Louise shared the bombshell news in the local park, with Vanilla Ice Cream man for company. What wasn't resolved was whether I would play any part in his life going forward. Eleven years later, with Peter aged 23, I was still waiting. He still didn't know that I was his father.

You would be forgiven for thinking, 'how is that possible?' The simple, but sad, answer is firstly, that I adhered to his mother's wishes, and secondly, the passage of time. Louise had decided that the upheaval would be too much for Peter and that his stability mattered more. I understood, believe me, but that didn't stop the gut-churning longing, day after day, as he grew up.

Occasionally, I met up with Lou, sometimes with Dawn, and on other occasions on my own. She updated me with regards to his progress at school and his hobbies, she would share the odd picture, and then I would return home, with the hurt and emotional emptiness palpable. Those encounters became less frequent, mostly down to Dawn discouraging me, due to the mental damage it was causing. My moods would always be challenging after a meet.

Withdrawn and snappy for a while, before day-to-day life took hold again.

I would see him sporadically at the local shopping centre, or in the park whilst walking Bonnie, and I would imagine just strolling up to him and introducing myself. I had similar reoccurring dreams where this scenario actually happened and we would end up hugging tightly. The clench only a father and son would recognise.

In 2006, they moved back to London. I don't have a great memory regarding dates but I remember that one. It was 30th April and Louise rang me in the morning to explain that a fantastic job offer had materialised, and it was time to go 'home'. That same morning, my beloved Bonnie died at the grand old age of eleven. I have had better days, to be honest.

Whilst Peter moving down to London didn't change anything, in reality, it did, for me. The old saying 'out of sight, out of mind' became all too familiar as the months and years passed. That was forgivable while he was still classed as a child and I stuck to Lou's instructions but, in 2008, when he turned eighteen, that was the opportunity to take the bull by the horns and get in touch. But I didn't. God, I thought about it. Every single day. But in the end, I was scared stiff. Frightened of rejection. Terrified that explaining the past would cause more damage, for him, Louise and myself.

Fast forward to March 2012, with a wedding set for October, and I had this overwhelming urge to try and get in touch with him, this total stranger, and invite him to the wedding. It was completely irrational but I was desperate for him to be by my side. I knew what this handsome (he had to be, didn't he?) twenty-three-year-old looked like as

Louise kept her promise and sent pictures and updates with how, and what, he was doing. I knew, for instance, that he had gone into the medical profession, like his mum. He was also a keen and bloody good sportsman, playing at a high level in both football and cricket. Like his dad.

Dawn constantly tried to dissuade me from contacting him. She was worried that my request to be his father after 23 years might not go as well as I seemed to expect.

"Jesus Christ, you haven't even sat down with the lad and had a bloody coffee yet," she said, one morning, as I brought the subject up for the umpteenth time.

"I know," I replied calmly, "but surely he would be tempted by a free trip to Italy? What a way to meet my side of the family. It would be kind of exotic."

"Knob," I heard her mutter, as she made her way to the front door, shaking her head. I think she was referring to me. She usually was.

Whatever advice was being dispensed, I wasn't listening and, as such, I made a call to Louise. The following exchange has been shortened for all our sakes.

"I'm thinking of getting in touch with Peter and asking him to the wedding. You okay with that?"

"Congratulations," she replied, with genuine cheeriness. "Of course, you can. That's your right, although I can't comment on how you will get on. He might embrace the opportunity. Or not."

"I understand that, but I do want to ask him. Does he know anything about me?"

Louise was quiet for a short time.

"A bit yes. Only because he has asked. More so recently. He knows your name, where you live, your family, and what happened."

"He knows he has a sister then? How did he react? Did you get the feeling he wanted to get to know me?"

"No. Not really, sorry. Anyway, give him a ring and take it from there. He's grown up now so he can handle himself. Got a good head on his shoulders."

Lou then proceeded to give me his mobile number.

"I will tell him you might call."

That conversation could have been taken two ways. Either he was starting to become inquisitive and was building up the courage to contact me. Otherwise, he was just curious and couldn't give a fig about me. I went with the former.

One evening, when Dawn was having an early dinner out with friends, and Charlotte was upstairs, I consumed the majority of a bottle of Chardonnay and made the call.

"Hi, Peter. It's your dad."

A bit forward, I grant you, and probably not the first words I had been rehearsing but that's what a bottle of vino can do to your freedom of expression. Feigned confidence I suppose.

"Hi," he replied. It was polite. He didn't sound surprised. But there was no excitement in that one word. Why would there be?

We had a bit of small talk. He told me a bit about his medical career and his sporting prowess. It was all rather stilted and clinical. The latter reminded me of his mother's persona from many years ago. Then I got round to the nitty-gritty.

"I know you don't know me at all, but I am getting married in October and I would like you to be there. I can come down to London, we could maybe have lunch or something, get to know each other before the wedding. It's in Italy, so I hope you have a passport."

That last sentence was both crass and a tad arrogant, as my thought process was that he was never going to turn down an offer as good as that.

"Thanks. Sounds like it will be a lovely day."

There was a long pause, and I could feel my heart beginning to race, ready for the confirmation of acceptance.

"I'm sorry. It's not for me, I'm afraid."

My stomach dropped. That same feeling you get when you ride on an Alton Towers' rollercoaster. A horrible, sickening feeling. I tried to gather my thoughts as Peter continued.

"No disrespect, but I am happy as I am. With Mum, my family and friends. You could have got in touch years ago, as I could have with you, but we didn't, did we? Must be some good reasons why. I don't think that should change, to be honest. Have a great wedding, enjoy your life as it is, as I will. I think that would be best for both of us. Thanks for the money by the way. It helped a lot with university. It was much appreciated."

I can't remember how I responded, and the money comment was a bizarre episode that will be explained later. I do remember saying, "Take care" before the phones disconnected.

I slumped back onto the sofa and stared at the mantelpiece. A framed picture of Dawn, Charlotte and myself stared back at me. Suddenly I felt confused as a couple of stray tears rolled down my cheeks. The one emotion that battled to the top, and stayed there, was one of relief. Don't ask me why. Five minutes before, I had been desperate for him to join me for my special day.

I made my way into the kitchen, opened another bottle and took a huge mouthful. Peter had made it quite clear he was happy with the status quo. He didn't want, or need, me in his life. He had also, I began to realise, released me from my own mental anguish. His words, "Enjoy your life as it is," kept reverberating around my brain. However harsh or wrong this sounds; I felt a burden had been lifted.

Dawn arrived home and we sat down in the kitchen.

"You have rung him, haven't you?" she asked, as she poured herself a glass.

"I did. No need to go into details but he won't be coming and we won't be in touch again. It's fine, honestly. Glad we had the chat though."

"I'm sorry," she said, as she got up, walked around the table and took my head into her chest. "I know you don't want to go into the detail but what are the headlines, so to speak?"

"He didn't say this but the best way of describing it would be summed up by one of your phrases."

"Which one?"

"You're a knob."

She smiled and pulled my head in closer and, as if by magic, Charlotte was with us, joining the cuddle, oblivious to what had just unfolded. This is okay I thought as we hugged each other.

This is more than okay.

Chapter Eleven:

Thanks to Justin Timberlake, I was now trawling through the Puglia area for a new venue. In the end, I decided to contact a wedding planner who lived there and, as such, knew all the secrets and nuances of that beautiful land. She offered us all sorts of ideas, including one that suddenly blew my socks off and became our fixation. A ceremony by the sea.

As they took us through the ideas and different options, Dawn and I felt this was perfect. Timberlake could do one. Whilst he would be stuck inside, surrounded by luxury and people waiting on him every second of the day, we would be outside, with the waves crashing against the rocks as we said our vows. Let's be honest though. I still would have liked to have been in Timber's shoes.

We had decided we would arrive for the ceremony by boat. At first, it was just the two of us but this was expanded to include the three bridesmaids Dawn had chosen and my best man. I have to admit that having Big Mac on a vessel didn't fill me with great confidence. Being the large specimen he was, I found myself double and triple checking with the planners, to confirm the size of the boat and what weight capacity it carried. They must have thought I was as mad as a box of frogs. Or had a bit of a weird hobby.

We sat back and let the experts get on with it. Hotels were booked, catering organised, everything you could think of apart from the clothes we were going to turn up in. Even that was half organised, for the men. We had a wedding outfitter all in place, with rough measurements taken for me,

Big Mac and my brother, Craig. The same offer had been extended to Dawn and her bridesmaids, but she had made it clear that her dress, and those of her party, would be chosen in good old Blighty, accompanying them to Puglia as if their lives depended on it. There is a world of difference between a groom choosing his wedding attire from a choice of three designs and the choice for a bride, which is inherently infinity and beyond.

As I was updating our plans to Big Mac one morning, he broached the subject of a stag do. Now I am going to level with you. I don't like them. I just don't understand the concept. I have been on a few and they are just another night out, with added debauchery, from what I have witnessed. Most of them feel forced, as though we should be doing something special, when the reality is that it is no different to a normal friends' get-together at a weekend. Well, apart from the fact that it might occur in the next town to create extra excitement.

I also abhor the sense that it is a last night of freedom. That the groom is encouraged to do something that he will regret the following morning, but which he feels is his duty to himself and his buddies to carry out. More recently, these testosterone excursions have morphed into whole weekends, weeks even. What's that about? Even more time for the groom to make a tit of himself, methinks, all with the baying encouragement of his so-called best friends.

One memory of being part of a stag do, and not in a good way, was the one I attended when I was in my late twenties. I was still living in the Dales, with my then-girlfriend, the volatile Susan. We weren't actually living together, as that would come later, but she stayed so often that we might well have been shacked up.

It was hard work just going on the darn thing. Susan never said I couldn't go; it was far more subtle than that. It was just the silence leading up to the event. The tense atmosphere she created. In the early months of our relationship, I just didn't go out with the lads at all. In a way, I had been manipulated into thinking that I didn't need to go, that the two of us was all I should need. I was okay with this at first and concurred. It felt more mature and grown-up. As time went by though, I missed just meeting up and having a laugh with some good friends. By the time I was invited on that particular stag do, I was getting braver. And quite possibly stupider.

The groom to be was a chap called Andy but everyone called him Pandy, which was self-explanatory I suppose. I didn't know him that well and I think I was invited due to knowing Big Mac and swelling the numbers a tad. The event was billed as 'Pandy's Magical Mystery Tour' and involved a bus. I think there were twenty-five of us that got on it that morning. Don't ask me how many crawled back on it at the end of the evening. I would hazard a guess it was a paltry single figure.

We met at the local Social Club at 9 am sharp. The landlord had opened it especially for us and had laid on some bacon sandwiches and a pint or two. Ridiculous. Look, I am not a party pooper, but anyone with half a brain would know that quaffing lager at breakfast time is not going to be helpful by the time you get to mid-afternoon, let alone late into the night. You will get there but heaven knows in what state. The responsible adult thing to do in this situation is to ask for an orange juice, so I asked for a pint of John Smith's.

At approximately 10 am, we loaded ourselves onto the bus, me a bit fuzzy in the head already and set off on Pandy's tour. I am not kidding you, but within two miles of setting off, some daft git asked the driver to pull over as he needed a piss. I ask you. What was the point? There then followed lots of shouting and singing as the bus headed towards our first destination.

When we pulled up at our first mystery destination, it was your standard pub stop. The venue was called The Bells, and I suddenly realised that this was not going to be a new mystery tour, with all the excitement of guessing where we were going at all. It was essentially the same route and same pubs we always went to when we had any 'do'. All the same journeys and places. That's the problem with the Dales. I did love it so much, but it was hard to find anything different to do. That was the only route where the pubs were in the right place, at the right times, so we always ended up at the same final destination. Bradford.

Once we arrived in the city, in the early evening sunshine, the group splintered into little factions. Pandy went off with a few of his close friends, not to be seen again, whilst Big Mac, a friend called Scully and I decided to go our own way and find some nice pubs and nightclubs. To be fair, the three of us were quite sensible in these situations. Whilst some will go hunting for 'ladies of the night', others to casinos or drug haunts, we kept it simple. Play some pool, down some tequila slammers, grab a curry, and end up dancing somewhere for a flirt with one or two female strangers.

Observing Big Mac on the dance floor was like watching the character Gareth, from Four Weddings and a Funeral. Manic with arms and legs everywhere. Similar size too. Scully and I watched this experience as we leant up against a crowded bar, Big Mac occasionally spotting us and exaggerating his body moves even more.

I always needed a few beverages before I hit any dance floor. Once on though, wild horses or even Big Mac couldn't drag me off. On this particular evening, I finally shuffled my way on as the nightclub started to thin out. Billie Jean had just come on, thumping through the speakers, and I was away with the birds. Or music in this case. I was dancing with Scully, who wasn't moving at all, just operating his feet, individually, a couple of inches either way. The poor lad just didn't have any rhythm in his body.

As I moonwalked my way across the dance floor, a young woman joined me to dance. I hazarded a guess she was in her early thirties. She had a lovely beaming smile, quite a loud coloured top on, which matched her voice when she started to talk. We all know how loud you have to speak when you are in a nightclub. In fact, it is nigh on impossible. You just can't hear each other. You could hear this girl though. Plain as day. She didn't have to get up close and shout in your ear, that's for sure.

As the magnificent Love Shack, by the B-52's, came on, she made her move on me. Or so my arrogant self was thinking.

"What's your friend called?" she asked, without raising her voice. Great. My vain bubble burst, just like that.

"That's Scully," I shouted, turning my head towards him, as he continued to dance, precisely, on the same spot.

We carried on dancing in lovely unison.

"No, not him. Your other friend. The maniac."

She looked in the direction of Big Mac, who was like a bloody octopus, sweating profusely, bouncing into anyone who got in his way.

"Oh, that's Big Mac. Why?"

"Can you introduce me, please? I have been watching him since you came in. He looks lovely but I feel a bit intimidated by his size."

I suppose it's a bit unfair, but I just had never contemplated any girl wanting to get to know him in that way. Don't get me wrong, he was and is lovely. He became my best man after all. It's just that I have never thought of him having a woman by his side. I couldn't think of anyone who could handle his big booming voice or presence. Having said that, this girl could certainly belt her words out.

"Yeh, of course," I shouted in her ear. "No need to be intimidated. He is just a giant pussycat. Honestly."

In a coincidence worthy of a rom-com, the resident DJ suddenly changed the mood into smooch mode. You will be familiar with that part of the evening. Last orders time, and if you were lucky, a harmless canoodle before you stagger off home. If you were single, of course. Big Mac was staggering back to the bar as 'It Must Have been Love' by Roxette began to reverberate around the room. I ushered the girl towards him and introduced them to each other. He was wiping his forehead, actually his whole head, with a handkerchief, as they started to chat. I went back to Scully who I found sitting all on his lonesome, at a table that had suddenly appeared as the club emptied.

As I made clear earlier on, the problem with having a pint at 9 am is that, by the time it's 2 am, you have forgotten where you are and that your bus had left an hour earlier. Whilst Scully and I started to panic, like Corporal Jones from Dad's Army, Big Mac was in deep conversation with Megaphone Milly.

Those were the days before mobile phones were readily available, or affordable, so when you promised your girlfriend, one that was not too understanding anyway, that you would be home at a certain time, the first thing you did was find a bright red phone box and let her know that you were safe and sound. You calmly stated that there had been a bit of a cock-up and you would be home soon, in your best sober voice, of course. Susan, on answering, was tranquil and broadly supportive, but I also knew from experience that the tone of her voice could lead to problems later.

We managed to find a taxi rank after a long search. Big Mac was still in deep conversation with the girl, who was not a particularly helpful companion by that time, and they had the obligatory hug and promise of keeping in touch as we coppered up to prove to the driver that we had the funds and made the long journey home.

Susan was still up as I quietly unlocked the front door, taking an age to close it behind me, trying not to make a sound of any sort. I had hoped she had given up the ghost for the night, to be honest. I slumped onto the sofa, took my belt off, and undid my jeans button to give some welcome space between waist and fabric. It can be a long day wearing pants that are always a size less than they should be. You know what I mean.

She was sat at the other end of the sofa and peered at me intently.

"Did you have a good night?" she asked, in a genuine sort of way. "Where did you end up?"

"Yeh, it was alright. Bradford as usual. We sort of split up when we got there so three of us stuck together for the rest of the night."

I took my shoes off, which was nearly as refreshing as the trouser manoeuvre.

"Who was with you?"

"Big Mac and Scully. They were on good form."

Susan rolled her eyes when the first name was said. She didn't have much time for my loveable giant.

We carried on chatting. I just tried to keep the conversation calm and simple so as not to give any ammunition that might alter the situation for the worse. In those circumstances, it was always a fine line. It was the next question she posed that started the problems that were about to surface.

"I got a bit of a whiff of perfume when you sat down. Charlie, I think. Cheap."

The 'cheap' word was the first inkling that it was about to go the wrong way, although I didn't have to think of an answer. No need to rack my brains. I knew where it had come from. The girl with the loud voice.

"That would be Megaphone Milly. Not her real name. Just the nickname I gave her," I said, smiling. "She wanted an introduction to Big Mac, so was shouting in my ear on the dance floor."

"Nobody wants an introduction to him," she snapped coldly.

"Well, it's true I'm afraid. Even Big Mac found an admirer. Shocked me too, to be honest, but there is someone for everyone they say."

I wearily got up from the sofa.

"Time for bed, I think. I am goosed."

I headed for the stairs and that is when the first blow occurred. Right across the back of my neck. It wasn't a hard object, more a whip feel. I turned around and could see she was brandishing my belt, just hanging there in her right hand, with the large steel buckle on show.

Two things popped into my head in that split second. One was to ensure that I bought the right size trousers in the future so that the belt never had to be removed, and the other was to her sheer premeditated callousness of her ensuring the hardest part of the belt was in place to do the optimum damage.

I turned on my heels and began running up the stairs, footsteps following me, the screams and shouts shuddering the walls. I was lucky, as most of the lashes that landed caught my legs or back. Thankfully, the bathroom was opposite the staircase, and I was in like a flash, door secured behind me. The only one that had a lock apart from the front and back doors.

Whilst I felt safe in there, the ensuing kicking, barging and general attacks on the door meant I didn't feel totally secure. After about half an hour, silence descended. I guessed, from previous experiences, that she had worn herself out. Exhausted, mentally and physically, I stayed awake for a while and then grabbed a couple of towels, got in the bath and went to sleep.

As I have stated before, the aftermath was always the same. Nothing was mentioned. My belt was lying on the landing and I picked it up and put it away in the drawer in the bedroom. I went downstairs and Susan was sat in the kitchen, sipping a cup of tea and nibbling on some toast, like butter wouldn't melt - pardon the pun. She said a cheery "morning" to me and I returned the compliment and grabbed a coffee from the pot. Madness. Pure and simple.

I look back and just don't understand. I cannot comprehend what happened and the acceptance that it was normal, even though I knew it wasn't. From then, to a year later, to actually plan to move in together … I'm sorry. I still don't have any answers. Well, I have one and her name is Dawn. Thank God.

I nearly forgot. The girl in the nightclub. Megaphone Milly. She is still with us. Her real name is Jenny and she and Big Mac have been together for twenty-five years and have been married for twenty. I don't believe in love at first sight but I will make an exception for those two.

In the end, it was a bloody good stag do I suppose. For them anyway.

Chapter Twelve:

Back to October 2012. Puglia. Or Apulia as it might be more commonly known. 'The heel of the boot' is the best description of this area in the South East of Italy. A region full of beautiful small towns, unique architecture, delicious cuisine, and for the week we were there, Justin Timberlake.

The arrivals for our wedding were scattered over the days leading up to the big day. We arrived on Monday 15th giving us a few days to ensure that all was in place for the Friday vows. The two respective families mostly landed on the Wednesday although one close auntie and uncle, who will remain nameless, had been out since the end of September. All right for some.

Dawn's bridesmaids travelled over together, that same Wednesday. Big Mac and his wife, Jenny, had actually arrived the day before us, citing some last-minute plans that needed addressing. He had requested that I kept Wednesday afternoon free, and although I reiterated that I didn't want, and wouldn't have, a stag do, he stated that he agreed entirely, but this was just a surprise for me and the lads.

The lads Big Mac was alluding to consisted of the two of us, my brother Craig, Spanish Kev, who I had invited at the last minute, and finally, Scully, who had become a good, if part-time, friend over the years. Big Mac called us 'The Five Musketeers', which didn't have the same ring to it as 'Three' to be honest. I presumed he had contemplated the 'Famous Five' tag but came to the same conclusion as me. It was a bit of a weird way to describe five grown men.

As we arrived in the lobby of the hotel for my surprise, the big man was standing outside, sunglasses on, a giant cigar hanging out of his mouth, his Godfather persona cemented forever. Out in the car park, we were greeted by a lovely man in glasses, who shook our hands and then gestured towards what was to be our fun for the afternoon. Scooters, or Vespas to be more accurate.

I will make another confession now that I hate anything on two wheels. A pushbike - far too much like hard work and does damage to my arse that can last for days. I had fallen off one badly, at the age of 12, when my front wheel had got stuck in a farmer's cattle grid. A motorbike - never been on one since I had a go on my brother's Yamaha 125 when I was about 16 and he let me give it a spin on a private road. Of course, I came off, resulting in me never going near one again. It might have been a different story if my first foray into biking had happened on normal tarmac but this stretch didn't just have gravel, it had bloody great boulders to navigate. I failed.

To say I was nervous would be an understatement but once again I couldn't say anything. This would require some sort of confrontation. No chance. It didn't help that Big Mac had a huge grin on his face and I could see the pride he felt with regards to the time, money and organisation he had spent on this special treat. The others were excitement personified, and they hurriedly picked the scooter they wanted. My brother raced over to the red one because he supported Liverpool and no other colour would do.

I suddenly noticed that there were only four scooters available when there were five of us but it didn't take long to realise that Big Mac wasn't going anywhere. I have no idea whether this was because he was scared, like me, or that the company didn't have a Vesta strong enough to take him out of the car park, let alone on a tour around the coast.

We did, of course, have a guide. A lovely chap called Roberto who advised that he would always lead, we just had to follow him and the excursion would be gentle and relaxed. I was sure that he meant well but Spanish Kev was a huge Formula One fan, had a monster bike himself, with a full leather outfit, and I just couldn't imagine him pottering away at 20mph for too long.

As we made our way out of the car park, Big Mac was looking on with that bloody cigar still clenched to his teeth and I was at the back of our small travelling group. Thankfully, we had a small quiet road before we hit the main carriageway so by the time we got there I had my weaving S-shape manoeuvres under control.

Whilst the main road was busy, we kept in a single file and tight to the curb. We soon turned off and before long we were bundling along the coast, and I began to relax and enjoy the ride. The views were breathtaking as we followed the sea and beautiful architecture. The Vespas were out in force as other groups passed us coming in the opposite direction, all waving and sounding horns. I was, by that point, having great fun.

At the start of the excursion, I stayed at the back of our group and kept my eyes firmly on the road in front of me. I also had the unsightly view of Spanish Kev's arse and bright yellow helmet as an added security. I could see our guide, Roberto, most of the time, up ahead and I suddenly realised that it was an experience I would never forget and wanted to take in every second.

We took a left turn at some traffic lights and began to travel away from the coast. I had lost close sight of Roberto but had Kev's yellow hard hat glistening in front so had little concern as we carried on our merry way. It was a couple of minutes later when three police outriders came up behind me that I got a bit spooked. They seemed to be pushing me along, refusing to overtake, and certainly not asking me to pull over. I had no choice but to speed up. This had the concertina effect of Spanish Kev having to do the same. He probably relished this unexpected speed opportunity but not me. I was now alongside him as we motored down the quiet road, still being harassed from behind.

I could see some Vespas up ahead and felt some relief. I expected to see just a couple as we slowed down, the police behind backing off, but as I got nearer, I could see dozens, all of them close together. As we got condensed, a large group of scooters set off and we joined them. You might think I was a bit thick, but I didn't really think anything of it, to be honest. I just thought it was all part of the tour. It was only when I realised that the police motorbikes were still behind me that I got a tad confused. Even more bewildering was when I spotted a further three outriders upfront, giving the impression they were keeping us all together. Which, of course, they were.

It was probably a further mile down the road, weaving our way around the bends, that my brain suddenly began to awaken. This might have been assisted by the fact that I had not seen another car, Vespa, or person coming in the opposite direction. Not one. Zilch. Minutes before, you couldn't have missed them. All I seemed to be doing, before joining our new group, was to wave or honk my horn as we made our way through the streets. Now, there was silence.

It didn't take much longer for the truth to out. We pulled into a large car park that was like a picnic beauty stop. It was empty, barring a huge, long table with a white cloth, housing what looked like ice-cold drinks and sandwiches. We got off our Vespas, removed the helmets and stretched our legs. I sidled up to Spanish Kev who was stretching his neck in all directions.

"Have you spotted Craig?" I asked, as I adjusted my shorts back into a comfortable position. "I can't see him."

"I haven't, or Roberto, for that matter," he replied, sweat dripping down his face. Something's not quite right. I have a feeling that we have joined a different group by mistake."

"Let's grab a beer," I said. "We might as well. We can ask one of them and take it from there."

I wasn't worried. It probably happened all the time and everything would get sorted and we would end up back at our hotel one way or another. I grabbed a cool beer and sat down next to a tall thin man, with grey hair and a fabulous, sculptured face.

"It's a beautiful area, isn't it?" I said, breaking the ice.

"It sure is," said the stranger, in a well-worn American accent. "Don't seem to recognise you from the hotel, so apologies."

"That's okay. I think there must have been different pick-up points and I wasn't paying attention."

He laughed.

"Too many beers, too soon maybe. So how do you know Justin?"

Have you ever had that feeling? A sudden realisation about something that was metaphorically staring you in the face. Mine was there. Right then.

The police riders, the absence of traffic. Unless I was very mistaken, we had, somehow, accidentally stumbled into Justin Timberlake's private Vespa excursion. Maybe it was his stag do. The Bradford tour, it certainly wasn't. I smiled at my new American friend, made the excuse that I needed the gents, and sauntered over to Kev. At the same time, I was, without arousing further suspicion, scouring the faces of my new Vespa buddies. It didn't take long to spot him. The quiff hairstyle still in place, despite being helmeted for God knows how long, and the neatly trimmed beard. It was him alright. He was laughing, amongst a small group, not a care in the world.

"You know what has happened?" I said to Kev, in an overly excited voice.

"Absolutely no idea, but not that bothered at the moment. I will just enjoy the beers for as long as they let us."

"I think we are sharing our scooter experience with Justin Timberlake. Not that he knows."

A salvo of beer shot out of Kev's mouth, like a raging waterfall.

"What the hell?"

For some reason, we still hadn't been rumbled. This was possibly due to the mass of riders moulding into one. They were just having a fun time and not expecting a couple of British idiots to infiltrate their private escapism. The police outriders may have some explaining to do at some point but we were just mingling. Actually, that is not strictly true. It was just me and Kev socialising. On our own, in a remote corner of the picnic park.

I decided to approach my new American acquaintance and come clean. He seemed like a decent chap and all I wanted to do was get the hell out of there with no harm done. I waited until he approached the gents, near to where we were situated, to spill the beans. I started to explain the situation.

"Jesus, man," he exclaimed, "that's just swell. Do you want to meet him?"

"Bloody hell, no," I replied. "We just want to get back to our hotel and not make a fuss, for him, the police. Everybody really."

"I get you. No probs. Leave it with me."

He wandered over to the police outriders and I watched as he explained the genuine mix-up. He then walked over to Mr Timberlake. My American friend was whispering in his ear and pointing towards us. There was just a moment when I thought Timbers was going to come over to us. He looked up in our direction and my heart did a little excited flip but then he nodded and turned away. To this day I am not sure if I felt a huge sense of relief or mass disappointment. My friend returned.

"The cops will take you back. Just get on your scooters and they will be ready to escort you to your hotel. Justin would appreciate it if you didn't say anything about this."

"Don't worry," I said truthfully, "just tell him that I signed an NDA ages ago. His secret is safe with me."

The American looked at me confused, as did Kev, as we walked quickly over to our Vespas. We got prepared and, before we knew it, we were out of the car park and heading back to our hotel. Escorted by two imposing police motorbikes, of course.

Back at the hotel, with Dawn reassured that I was safe and sound, I wandered down to the pool where Big Mac was lying in the deep end as though he was in a giant bath. His arms were stretched over the sides, another cigar perfectly placed in his mouth, sunglasses on as usual. In essence, he looked like he owned the place.

"Have a good time?" he asked, in his big booming voice, as he chewed away on the stub.

"It was brilliant, thank you. You have no idea how special it was. I will tell you when I have more time. Probably after the wedding. Be safer then."

He took his sunglasses off and looked at me quizzically. I smiled and headed for the outside bar.

I know I said I didn't like stag dos, but I will make an exception for mine. It certainly was very good.

Chapter Thirteen:

Thanks to the local wedding planner, our big day required little input from us. No last-minute rushing around or crises to be dealt with. Everything was in place and we had a final debrief the day before, by the sea. I can think of worse places for a meeting. By and large, we just had to get dressed in our chosen outfits and nosy on down to the coast where our boat would be waiting to take us the short journey to our 'crashing by the waves' ceremony.

Unlike the Spanish wedding debacle where I impersonated Charlie Caroli for over twelve hours, this time my suit fitted me perfectly. I know it's a tad conceited but as I looked in the mirror, I did see a bloody good-looking, well-dressed chap staring back at me. One that would make any mother proud. I did overlook the baldness, the crooked nose from a footballing accident, and the slightly protruding stomach, but as the character Reg says in the Life of Brian, "All right, but apart from the…"

I hadn't seen Dawn or Charlotte all morning. We had agreed to some traditions being left intact and one was not to see each other the night before, until she walked up the 'aisle' in the afternoon. That part was soon abandoned when we remembered that we were all boarding a boat together. I did suggest that we could place her head in a sack to hide her identity until we got there, but this was dismissed with her usual response of, "You're a knob."

In the end, it was agreed that we would all meet at the hotel bar at noon, on the dot. Everyone was invited but I wasn't bothered about general family and friends as long as Dawn, her three bridesmaids, Charlotte and Big Mac were on schedule so that we would be on time for the short car journey to our vessel.

The sporadic arrival of the main players was a sight to behold, and I mean that in a 'tears in your eyes' emotional type of way. The first to arrive as I stood at the bar was Charlotte. She bounded up to me in her stunning aubergine coloured dress. She twirled around, in her element, grinning from ear to ear. If ever I needed a reminder of how lucky I was, that was a good moment. The three bridesmaids soon followed, in identical frocks, all looking lovely, proud, and ready for the day ahead.

Big Mac was next. He wasn't late as such, but it would have been nice if he had been by my side when I arrived at the bar, instead of yours truly looking like a right spare one. I have to admit that it wasn't easy getting a morning suit that was designed to fit the big fella. The local outfitters had achieved miracles as I watched him stride towards me. He didn't look too bad, all suited and booted.

Finally, as we sipped a drink and conversed together, Dawn entered the room. I have no idea why she didn't come with the others, or if anything had happened, but there she was, smiling broadly as she approached me. I apologise now to all female readers but, as you have gathered by now, I am a man. I have no idea how to describe her dress, suffice to say it was cream in colour, simple in design, and looked phenomenal.

We said our goodbyes to the family contingent, told them not to be late as they ordered another drink from the bar. We loaded ourselves into a blacked-out car, like some strange finalists of The Apprentice, and drove down to the coast.

The boat which the planners had organised was a large motor one, with a skipper to guide us to our ceremony. I have no idea what the technical terms are for those beautiful vessels but suffice to say it was probably a bit large for the seven of us. We also had an onboard host to look after us, doubling up as our wedding photographer.

There was plenty of room to sit at the front and soak in the October sunshine. There was also a nice shaded area with lots of seating near where our captain would be, and finally, below deck, where there was a table, seats and even a couple of beds, if required. As the journey was less than twenty minutes, I was pretty sure that the latter wouldn't be required, as it would have been a bit rude for the bride and groom to consummate prior to saying their vows, let alone abandoning their close friends for a quickie. It was also highly unlikely that we would have used the front deck either, due to the attire we were wearing, but essentially, we had everything we needed, including the complimentary champagne on ice.

We made ourselves comfortable and our spirits, understandably, were extremely high. There was a huge amount of laughter as our host looked after us, clicked his camera and ensured that corks were popped. Meanwhile, our skipper prepared us for departure. The seven of us were clinking flutes and sipping away, with even Charlotte allowed just the smallest glass of bubbles. It couldn't have been any better.

We set out to sea and our small group splintered away to explore the different parts of our beautiful vessel. Big Mac headed to the front, which shouldn't have surprised me, but I did have a quiet word with both the host and captain with regards to my concern that he could tip us downwards like a scene out of Titanic, meaning arse up. After a quizzical look from both of them, followed by a heartily laugh, I got the reassurance needed and let him roam freely, with the obligatory cigar glued to his teeth.

The rest of us stayed in the middle of the boat, sipping champagne, until two of the bridesmaids decided to go down below. They were best friends of Dawn, sisters, born eighteen months apart from each other. Thick as thieves, they never seemed to leave each other's side. This had prompted us to tease them that they must be twins as it was quite uncanny how identical they were in looks and build. The last of the bridesmaids, Julie, decided to join Big Mac at the front. We nearly had a catastrophe when she started to clamour up the side, still in her high heels, until the host spotted her and handed her some complimentary flip flops that were onboard for us, if required.

As we trundled along, waving at other boats and people on the coast, our host requested us all to gather for some photographs. Big Mac and Julie made their way back to the middle whilst Dawn shouted down below for the two sisters to join us. Silence. She shouted again. Still no response. We then enlisted Charlotte to pop down and see what they were up to. Finally, Charlotte reappeared up the tight steps with the sisters not far behind.

"Dad," Charlotte said, as she snuggled in between Dawn and me. "I need to tell you something."

"In a minute, sweetheart. We need to listen to the man so that we can get these photographs done."

I bent down and gave her a little kiss on the cheek.

We got into two lines. Big Mac stood behind me with the two sisters on either side. They were quite tall, in addition to looking alike, so had the right balance for the required look. Dawn and I stood in front, holding hands, with Charlotte to my left, and the other bridesmaid, Julie, stood next to the bride-to-be. We were all in place, laughing and teasing each other, when the boat made a small turn and we all unbalanced momentarily. There were a few 'oohs and aahs' as we steadied ourselves, trying to hold our positions. It was at this point that I felt a sort of wetness land on my shiny bald head. For a split second, I thought it was a wave from the sea or a bird dropping but as I put my hand up to wipe it away, it felt warm, and even worse, lumpy.

I quickly turned around, which in hindsight was the wrong thing to do, as a rather large swathe of sick hit my face, and even worse, the front of my black morning suit. The bridesmaid sister, situated right behind me, had honked. Twice. As I stood, frozen to the spot, from the corner of my fluid-obstructed eye, I saw the second sister let her mouthful of vomit leave her lovely mouth and hit Dawn. All over the back of her hair.

Although it was too late, Big Mac swung into action and quickly turned one sister, followed by the other, so that they were facing the sea, bending over the side to continue their retching. I'm not sure how to describe the next few minutes. Dawn screamed loudly, Big Mac was in the middle of the two sisters, tapping their backs as though he was winding a couple of infants, and Charlotte was tugging on the bottom of my suit jacket.

"I was trying to tell you, Daddy. They have been sick on the bed downstairs."

Important lesson learnt. Don't ignore your child when they want to tell you something. I would have to deal with that situation later as more pressing concerns needed addressing. A bride and groom covered in vomit for starters.

Our host, and part-time photographer, was motionless. I had a feeling that he had not dealt with this type of crisis before. A groom with a scattered yellow mass dripping from the lapels of his jacket, and a bride with a similar concoction embedded in her carefully moulded hair. Then he got his phone out and started to make frantic calls.

"Looks like they suffer from seasickness then," I said to Dawn, as we sat staring into space, waiting for the instructions that are our host had advised would be forthcoming.

"I had no idea," she replied, quietly. "They never said anything."

"You didn't think to ask?" I queried, as I took my jacket off and threw it as far away as possible, the warm air making the stench unbearable. "I made sure Big Mac was happy with the idea."

"Christ. Big Mac would be happy if you told him we were getting married on a bungee jump."

"True," I replied, as I put my arm around her, the smell from her hair getting worse as the sun started to dry out the human fluid. "But at least I knew. Not often I can say this to you but I will make an exception today. You really are a knob."

She looked at me and a small smile gently materialised as she rested her head on my shoulder, which was not ideal to be honest.

Our host came over and sat with us to take us through his proposed solution. Our captain was still steering us to our destination. Big Mac was still caring for the sisters as they were draped over the side of the boat, whilst the other bridesmaid, Julie, entertained Charlotte. The upshot was that a new jacket would be there for me on arrival and a mobile hairdresser for Dawn. You couldn't have asked for a better service, given the circumstances.

As we finally moored, we saw our families and friends relaxing at the private bar, oblivious to what had just occurred. Stepping off must have been one heck of a sight for any onlookers. I looked okay although the baby wipes hadn't quite done the job and there were a few dried signs on my face and shirt. Dawn was worse, her auburn hair looked like it had yellow highlights in it. The two sisters were tightly held by Big Mac, looking like they had seen the ghost of all ghosts. They woozily stepped off the boat, hanging on to him for dear life.

Within a few minutes, Dawn was sorted. I say sorted. She had a brand-new style that was sort of spiky, like the singer Pink from the early noughties. The best our emergency hairdresser could do in reality. I had my new jacket, which was slightly tighter, restricting any urgent movement, left or right. Not ideal. Meanwhile, the two bridesmaids were gulping water down, whilst our host and guide did his best to wipe the dresses clean of their own spew.

The walk down the man-made aisle was beautiful, if a little stressful. I made my way slowly, with Big Mac, under the impression that everyone knew what had happened and they were looking at me, whispering and pointing. They weren't of course, it was just my mind playing tricks.

Dawn followed, a couple of minutes later, to a piece of music called Vesper, from the James Bond film, Casino Royale, that cascaded across our open venue. I glanced back, taking a peek at my bride-to-be, and she looked beautiful. The pointy hair did look a bit odd but otherwise it was all as I had envisaged. Well, apart from the staggering bridesmaids behind her who were wobbling one way and another, and could hardly stay on their feet.

The ceremony was beautiful. As we said our vows we could see and hear the waves gently crashing against the nearby rocks, which was a welcome relief from the endless gurgles and burps coming from the bridesmaids, close behind us. The moment we both said 'I do' was emotional and slightly surreal. Facing each other, our hands clasped together, grinning from ear to ear, we had finally done it. Nearly a dozen years in the making. The long journey from our first meeting in my tardy green suit, when Dawn took that instant dislike to me and then, thankfully, thawed to love me, unconditionally. Even the odd whiff of stale vomit couldn't spoil that moment.

The reception was held in a giant marquee and was far too big for the thirty of us. Having said that, it suited us fine, especially Big Mac, who had all the room he needed to show off his flailing dance moves. The majority of our family and friends went out of their way to compliment Dawn on her daring, jagged hairstyle, expressing their amazement at how it had changed from the hotel to the ceremony. They honestly thought she had done it deliberately, to surprise them all at the last minute. We didn't have the heart to tell them. Not until months later anyway. We had also promised the sisters that we wouldn't say anything, as they felt embarrassed enough. What happened on the boat, stayed on the boat.

When I first walked off that vessel, all those years ago, all I could think of was how unlucky we were, ill-fated. Today, we laugh uncontrollably at the memories, helped by our host and self-styled wedding photographer who, unbeknown to us, had kept clicking away as the mayhem unfolded in front of him. Some of the pictures he took were both hilarious and mortifying and he will never know how grateful we are now for his indiscretion. We keep them in a separate album, our own private one, entitled Our Hapless Wedding.

How could we have called it anything else?

One Bizarre Death

Chapter One:

I am acutely aware that writing about death is tricky. It stirs deep emotions and memories that can be upsetting, especially when it involves someone close to you. I didn't think this had happened to me, but it had, albeit a long time ago.

This sad event involved my grandma and I was seventeen years of age. The memories of her passing are sketchy, which is fine by me, as I get to remember her alive, full of life, and the best grandparent anyone could hope for. I was, unfortunately, the first one from our family to be informed, the day she died. That was a horrible twist of fate as my mum was on holiday, and the police couldn't get hold of my older brother, Craig, so yours truly was next in line.

Most of the day's events are cloudy and buried deep in my subconscious. I struggle to remember traumatic events, which is odd. I just seem to have an ability to forget, or just find my stiff upper lip, and crack on with life. It can't be healthy though, and I do worry that one day some event will come along, a death probably, that I can't cope with, that I won't be able to just brush aside. That does frighten me a tad.

When my grandma passed, whilst I felt sad, I don't remember grieving. I much preferred to think and talk about her life and laugh heartily. How she was an unintentional spoonerism expert. Olympic standard I would say. I would go to her flat for dinner where she would announce proudly that we were having 'chork pops'. She adored the Royal

Family and would talk about 'our queer old dean'. She detested politicians and would shout at the TV whenever they appeared, exclaiming that they all told a 'lack of pies'. I could go on, but you get the idea.

My all-time memory, and there were many, was one particular Christmas Day. For some reason that I cannot recall, she ended up spending the day with me, my younger sister, Jess, and elder brother, Craig, at his house. I have no idea where Mum was that particular year, as she and Grandma usually spent Christmas together. Anyway, the three of us shared the cooking, with yours truly in charge of the turkey, whilst Grandma relaxed with a sherry or two. We had a wonderful time. The wine flowed, and Grandma was brimming with fun and laughter. We loved to play board games and she had always been at the forefront of that ritual. That particular year, Craig had bought a game called Bizzy Buzzy Bumbles.

The premise was simple. You wore individual magnetic Buzzy Bumbles headbands and all you had to do was keep bobbing your head up and down and collect the magnetic bees from the board. The winner was the one who collected the most, and it was, primarily, a free-for-all until complete. Bearing in mind that Grandma was in her eighties, I approached Craig quietly.

"Do you think it's a good idea to play this particular game?" I asked. "It is a bit physical."

"She will be fine, I think. I'd better ask her, shouldn't I?"

Craig went off to ask and came back into the kitchen with an affirmative.

"She is up for it. I knew she would be. This is going to be cracking fun." And with that, he was away to prepare the table.

He was right of course. She was up for it, as usual. It was quite a sight, seeing the four of us, tight around a small table, violently bobbing our heads, and crashing into each other as we tried to obtain the bees. A completely ridiculous pastime but when you are full of wine, with a grandma acting like a teenager, it was wonderful and very, very funny.

We had planned that one of us would accompany Grandma back to her flat no later than 7 pm as we knew she would tire, but she was still going strong after midnight, pleading for one more 'Busty Bees game'. It was me who finally got her coat and escorted her the short distance home. We linked arms as we walked. She was so happy that evening. Spending time with her grandchildren was special to her. A constant in our lives from birth upwards, she entertained us royally for many years, and with more love than you can imagine.

It was the following day, when Mum called us with the news that Grandma had been to the local accident and emergency and was in a neck brace for at least a fortnight. Mum wanted an explanation as the old girl wasn't saying anything. She was no snitch, that's for sure. At first, Mum was annoyed at us for putting her at risk, until she heard all the details and calmed down. She reluctantly agreed with us that Grandma just wanted to live life and be herself, especially at eighty plus. Who knew how much longer we would have that special woman in our lives?

The good news was that we got another ten years with her. The bad news was that final day. The one we knew was coming, sooner or later. I do remember seeing her lying on her living room floor. I think she had a smile, but as my memory won't allow me to access it to see if this was true, I will keep that visual. It helps.

The thing is, the family upset didn't last long. That's not being callous, but just the reality with an older person, however much you love them. You half-expect it as the days, months, and years go by. You start to cherish the moments together knowing that it could be your last shared experience. I am okay with that, and the feelings I had when she passed. I much prefer thinking about the hugs, the spoonerisms, and the 'busty bees', to be honest.

The funeral was a small and understated event. Mum had asked one of us if we could sing Grandma's favourite song at the funeral service. As a budding 'am-dram leading man', I confidently volunteered. How I wish I hadn't. The song in question was from a German opera called Das Land des Lächelns, written in 1929, with the tune of 'You are my Heart's Delight'. I'm not convinced you can access it on Spotify but you are welcome to look it up. It was impossible to sing, by me anyway.

We didn't have the luxury of a resident pianist at the crematorium who could knock it down a few octaves for me. All we had was a backing track that Craig had engineered, that minimised the original singer's tenor voice. As my little rocks had dropped a few years earlier, I was definitely in the bass category which put me at a slight disadvantage. If I had still been that ten-year-old angelic choir boy, I would have been just fine.

I butchered it. Pure and simple. I had listened to it and practised the song, countless times. In the bedroom, shower, and even at work but, crucially, only in my head. Whilst it sounded challenging and I had never sung it out loud, I honestly thought I would be okay, until the actual funeral unfolded, that is. I don't think I sang a note in tune, or at the right pitch, for that matter. The congregation was very kind and smiled at me, more in sympathy I imagine but, by the second verse, it was pretty obvious that I needed to stop. Craig was making a slitting movement across his throat, whilst Mum was wide-eyed and open-mouthed, not in admiration I assumed.

I stopped and put my hand up, to motion that I couldn't go on. I ensured that this was communicated clearly, that I was too upset to continue, and that it was all too much for me. The reality was that my attempt was awful and embarrassing. Best to keep the myth that I could sing intact, I thought, as I slowly walked back to my seat. I had a reputation to keep up, after all. No idea what it was, but we all had one as a teenager, didn't we?

Writing about my grandma has brought back so many happy memories. I realise that I miss her dearly. I hope she is looking down, smiling and bobbing her head. Hopefully, she will be satisfied that I finally became successful in work and life, with an inspiring wife and beautiful daughter. I hope I made her proud. In the end.

Chapter Two:

We all behave differently when we are informed about the death of someone we know. It depends on who it is, of course, and there will be differing reactions whether it be a close family member, a friend or a colleague. In addition to these are the famous or celebrities who pass away. Not those that are half-expected, due to old age or issues we might be familiar with, but those that are taken from us far too young, the unexpected ones that shake us individually and in some cases, the world.

The most famous one in recent times was, of course, Princess Diana. I shall come back to this extraordinary figure later, but I also seem to have a thing about musicians and singers that leave us far too early. Whitney Houston's death upset me in 2012, but I couldn't tell you why. I didn't particularly like her music although The Bodyguard was, and still is, one my guilty pleasures.

David Bowie was another. I hadn't really appreciated his music, but his death in 2016 genuinely resonated with me, probably because even though I thought most of his music was garbage, his soundtracks had followed me through my childhood and teenage years, subconsciously. I have changed my mind since, I promise you. Too young to appreciate him, I think. The man was a genius.

Michael Jackson's death jolted me in 2009, mostly because I, or anybody else for that matter, was not expecting it. However, as I worked away that day, I assumed the snippets I kept getting from the radio were for General Michael

Jackson, the retired Chief of the General staff of the British Army. I only got the gist when I returned home in the evening. In a way, I got a double shock that day, as I was quite sad for the General in those hours when I had mourned the wrong chap.

It's strange what the mind can do. I can't remember the details of my daughter Charlotte's birth, but can recall exactly what I was doing, and when, the day John Lennon died in 1980. I was thirteen and I remember learning about his sad demise whilst getting some sherbet dips from the local post office and seeing a newspaper headline: 'We Loved You, Yeah, Yeah, Yeah'. I was in a daze for weeks.

There are those, like John Lennon for me, that you remember everything. Exactly where you were when you found out. You will all have at least one, we all do. Whilst rather recent, the death of George Michael, on Christmas Day 2016, is etched in my memory. Dawn was getting ready for bed and Mrs Brown's Boys had just ended. Thank God. Did someone say comedy? Anyway, I was laying on the sofa when I heard the high-pitched scream from upstairs. I raced to the bottom of the stairs to see her sat at the top, in tears, mobile in hand.

"Turn the news on. George Michael is dead."

I raced back and put the news on. She was right. This one hit me very hard. Similar to Bowie, but with music I liked, George had been with me through the eighties, nineties and finally the noughties. He was my soundtrack, with accompanying love life, for over thirty years. I remember dancing to 'Wham' with Louise in London, enjoying the album 'Older' on my own, with headphones on, as Susan preferred 'What's the Story Morning Glory' which meant I was banned from playing George out loud. Then, finally, I recall cuddling up with Dawn and embracing the beauty of 'Patience' in 2004. I think I did suffer from genuine grief. Not that I told anyone.

The one we are all familiar with, regarding the night they died, was Diana, Princess of Wales. I defy anyone not to access that memory. Go on, do it now. You remember, don't you? My memory is so clear with regards to that evening and early morning. It does, for bad measure, also involve my then-girlfriend, the now infamous Susan.

The year was 1997, the date 31st August. I was, at the time, living with Susan and my retriever, Bonnie, in our rented house. At the same time, my new work colleague, and ultimate saviour, Dawn, was becoming a feature in my life day-by-day. It was around this time that my thoughts were beginning to think of a better life, away from Susan and the toxic, fearful relationship I had got myself into.

I remember that it was a Saturday evening and Susan and I had attended a friend's 25th birthday party at the local rugby club. I had come to dread those types of events. The memories of country homes and stag do altercations, alongside a few other scenarios, had made me wary, if not scared, of anything we got invited to, wondering what might happen at the end of the night.

The evening itself was great fun, with a huge amount of dancing to some great 1980s music. Our local DJ had not got around to updating his set, or had any new records for that matter, but that was okay with me. I know I drank a lot that evening, far too much to be honest. In those days I could go from pints of beer, a gentle manoeuvre to gin and tonic, and end on a glass of wine or two when I felt a bit bloated.

The sad thing was that I only drank this much for two reasons. One was to have as little memory as possible in case the worst happened later, and secondly, to cushion the pain if it did.

On arriving home, well after midnight, I did what I always did and collapsed on the sofa and turned the TV on. It felt like a comfort blanket in those moments, that it would, in some way, stop any argument she might have been storing up on our walk home. It worked this time, as Susan quietly grabbed a glass of water from the kitchen and headed upstairs in silence. I know that my body and mind instantly relaxed. The window of conflict had passed.

I hadn't been paying attention to the TV until she had disappeared, as my senses had been on red alert. My eyes suddenly focussed as I started to watch what was a breaking news report which involved the Princess. I increased the volume and sat upright from my drunken stupor. I could understand some of what was being said. A car accident, Paris, hospital, all mentioned by a reporter somewhere in France.

This potential, shocking, event sobered me up immediately. Odd how that happens, isn't it? No idea how it materialises, which is a pity, as it would be a good money-spinner for the person who found out how. I shouted at Susan to come downstairs. I'm not sure why, in hindsight. I suppose it's an instinct when you are sharing your life with someone, that seismic events like that need to be shared, even if the said relationship had other problems.

"Sue. Are you coming down? Princess Diana has had a car accident. Not sure how bad yet, but I have a nasty feeling it's not going to be a good outcome."

I had no idea why I thought this at the time. The reports were sketchy, mentioning broken arms, etc. but it was because there was so much speculation that I had an uneasy feeling it was worse than the correspondents were reporting. Susan appeared at the bottom of the stairs; arms folded, looking disinterested at the TV in the corner.

"Do you think she is dead?" she asked, coldly.

"Don't know but something's not right," I replied, as she stood there motionless. "The coverage seems too detailed for a broken arm."

"You're going to stay up, aren't you," she said, shaking her head, "until you know what has happened?"

"Too right I am. Come and sit down. Watch it with me."

I was by then sat, rigid, concentrating on every word coming out of the screen.

"This is huge news."

"To be honest, I'm not bothered either way," she sighed. "I know it's only because you fancy her. You're a bit sad to be honest, so I will leave you to it."

Susan made her way towards me, slapped me hard across the back of my head and departed back up the stairs.

That was the pivotal moment for me. As I sat there, watching the events unfold, my mind also made the decision that I had to get out of there. It was three hours before the dreaded, and sad, announcement came that the Princess had died, and in all that time I was scared that Susan would come back down the stairs and start a confrontation. I hadn't had that before. Usually, the abuse or violence started immediately. I never had time to think about it, just dealt with the consequences the best I could. The unknown anticipation was more frightening.

I cried when the newsreader solemnly addressed us all watching that night. I still believe my tears were for Diana, but they were also for me. For who I was, what I had become, and the terrifying relationship I had let myself become involved in.

As I bowed my head in respect, I also prayed, in my own way, that Dawn would take me away from all this. Forever.

Chapter Three:

As you are aware, if you have been following the bits and pieces of my life, I worked at a hotel for a while in the beautiful Yorkshire Dales. It was a popular establishment with half a dozen bedrooms, a dining room serving à la carte, and a posh bar that served the best beers in the area, courtesy of yours truly cleaning and sampling them most mornings at 9.30 am sharp. There was also a large open area that served 'bar snacks'. Do you remember that description? I think we call it lunch, dinner, or 'going for a meal' now.

We were also famous for our funeral teas, but then we were the only local venue that could pack a hundred people in for a beer and a sandwich. We were very good at them though, and whilst death avoided me on a personal level, I did see many a grieving family while I was there. I learnt very quickly how to adjust my raucous personality to fit the circumstances, as the wake could be very emotional and raw, or just one giant jamboree without balloons or party poppers.

Our small town heaved with tourists in the summer as it was the perfect rest stop on the way to the Lake District. That was before a bypass was built that basically killed all the trade stone-dead. I worked in the hotel before, and after this seismic change, and the difference was stark. Overnight, it became a ghost town. To be fair, it was probably the kick-up-the-arse I needed to evaluate my working life and start to plot that elusive escape route.

The hotel part of the business continued to thrive but, due to the drop-off in general trade, the staffing levels had diminished by two thirds and those that were left behind doubled up on chores. I was Front of House Manager at the time and, under me, I had a couple of bar staff and waiters. One of them was Spanish and had been at the hotel since he was a young eighteen-year-old. I have no idea how on earth Miguel came to be at the hotel, or the Yorkshire Dales for that matter, but he was part of the furniture and very popular with the locals and our regular tourists.

One of the doubling-up tasks was cleaning the bedrooms. This became my added area of responsibility, along with Miguel. Every morning, we had to clean the bar, the 'bar snack' area and the dining room, followed by any bedroom that had been occupied the night before. All before 11 am. Bonkers when I look back, but we did it, which was mostly down to Miguel. He was manic. In personality and work ethic. He could deploy two hoovers at once. He could clean and change the sheets in a bedroom in under fifteen minutes, however soiled they were.

Our landlord and boss was an old-fashioned type of chap. All country attire and pipes. He loved the finer things in life, lived in a large house away from the hotel, and had made a pretty good living out of it. He had, though, grown tired of it all, especially when the town resembled the abandoned island James Bond visited in Skyfall. The only buzz he got was if any VIPs made a reservation to stay. That had become rarer, but the likes of a former Home Secretary, a few famous actors, Terry Wogan and a rather lovely journalist, from the now-defunct TV Times, had all frequented our quaint little inn from time to time.

He was, therefore, a tad giddy when we got a call, followed by a reservation, from a Lord Brocklehurst. He advised that he would be arriving on a Thursday evening, departing the following Monday morning. He required dinner, bed and breakfast and was travelling alone. Our landlord went into overdrive. Every corner of the hotel was checked for dust. The bedrooms were filled with flowers for His Lordship's arrival, as we were instructed that he might choose any of the rooms, even if they were already occupied. We all wore ties on duty anyway, but we were ordered to wear jackets for the duration of his stay. It was so over-the-top but typical of our boss in those situations.

I was on duty when His Lordship arrived. He was a lovely man, mid-fifties at a guess, with a beautifully manicured moustache. He was dressed immaculately and spoke softly in a posh, old-fashioned type of voice. He oozed the epitome of high society. I checked him in and took him upstairs so that he could choose his bedroom. I was like an estate agent showing him around each one, outlining the benefits so he could make an offer, sorry, an informed choice.

He also liked the finer things in life. Lunch was a three-course event, with a very expensive wine to complement it. Dinner was always à la carte, the best fillet steak, washed down with a top-of-the-range red. He would sit at the bar, from 11 am, drinking brandies like they were going out of fashion and we would chat away in-between me serving other guests and diners. He was fascinating to listen to, with his stories of royalty and the circles he moved in. The landlord graced us with his presence every evening, just so that he could spend an hour in His Lordship's company. More liquors consumed. All on the good Lord's tab.

By Sunday night, we had run out of brandy. And his favourite wine, red or white. Our head chef had made an emergency dash to the local farm shop to stock up on fillet steak. The Lord was relentless. If this was his style of living, I thought to myself, he will be dead in the not-too-distant future. He certainly needed a salad now and again, preferably with orange juice.

His last evening advanced into the early hours of Monday morning. We had, what we called in those days, a lock-in. Lord Brocklehurst presided over this illegal venture with half a dozen of our favourite, and most trustworthy, customers. The lights were dimmed in case a passing policeman peered through the curtains. Fat chance. You would have got better odds on Lord Lucan turfing up than seeing a boy in blue.

He chatted away. His royal stories got more outlandish as the hours passed by. Discretion was not his middle name, to be honest. The locals were lapping it up, even more so when the drinks kept coming, courtesy of our special guest. By the time we wrapped up at 3 am, he was rather pissed, his new friends plastered, and yours truly, sozzled. Not great news when you are on breakfast duty at 6 am, I can tell you.

I made it on time. Don't ask me how but, after a while, you do get used to these types of evenings and you get rather immune. We had three bedrooms occupied that Sunday night. Alongside the Lord, we also had two couples staying. One was a young pair of newlyweds on their honeymoon. I never saw them, but that was understandable in the circumstances. The other couple was elderly and they were there to walk. Over the Three Peaks, and then back again. I wish I had that outdoor love in me. I might have stayed and embraced the surroundings more.

They all came down for breakfast in good time but, by 9 am, His Lordship had not yet surfaced. Not surprising really. It was not for us to wake him, until 11 am, when it was checking-out time. We carried on with our morning routine, cleaning and preparing for opening as usual. By 11 am, he still hadn't stirred so I rang the landlord for advice, to be told, in no uncertain terms, not to wake him.

By mid-afternoon, it was getting ridiculous. I know he was a Lord, but we needed to get in that room and clean it ready for the next guests. We were fully booked for Monday night so something would have to give. I tried to get hold of the landlord again but couldn't track him down, so it was time to make a managerial decision.

I collected the spare key from the kitchen and took Miguel for support. Once upstairs, we knocked gently on his door. Then louder. If I had had a police-battering ram to hand, I would have had a go with that to try and wake him up. No sound. In the end, I made the choice to enter the room. We sort of tiptoed in, putting our heads around the door.

He was lying peacefully on the bed. Flat out on his stomach, his face deep into the pillow, the white sheets covering him. I decided to say something, more in a whisper than out loud.

"Lord Brocklehurst. It's after 2 pm, Sir."

Nothing. No movement at all.

"He is dead," said Miguel suddenly. "I can tell."

I looked at my Spanish colleague in horror.

"He can't be!"

Miguel wandered over to the bed and grabbed his hand from under the sheets. He waved the arm up and down.

"See. He is dead."

It was one hell of a shock I can tell you. I hadn't had any training for this. I had no idea what to do. I made the quick decision to leave the room and lock it. Then what? I went downstairs to the reception area and found his reservation form. It had an address on it but no contact telephone number. Nobody to ring. That was not our normal procedure but then he was a Lord, after all, so I hadn't checked anything properly. I decided to ring the landlord, who after a period of silence, spoke quietly.

"You need to ring the police."

"Why?"

"It is classed as an unexplained death, so they need to be informed. I am coming over now."

The police duly arrived and took over the whole of upstairs. We just carried on with as normal a service as possible. I won't lie, it was quite exciting as more and more officers turned up. Some in uniform, others not. I had no idea that it required so many officers to sign off an unexplained death, but then I had no idea what they needed to check for.

It was at least 48 hours later when an officer requested a meeting with us and we all met in the main dining room, with doors closed, like the final scene out of an Agatha Christie mystery.

There was good and bad news. The good news was that he had died of natural causes and probably suffered a heart attack. Not a surprise was it? The bad news was that he had no next of kin and his name wasn't Lord Brocklehurst. In fact, he wasn't even a Lord.

"I beg your pardon," I said, suddenly taking notice of what had just been said.

"I am sorry," the officer continued, "but the guy was just a conman. A trickster. He is wanted by most police forces around the country, for something or other. He just kept changing his identity so nobody could actually pin him down."

I could see the blood draining from my boss by the second, his teeth gripping his pipe very tightly.

"That can't be possible," I countered. "He knew so much about the Royal Family. The detail, everything. You can't just make that stuff up."

"He was good, wasn't he?" the officer half-smiled. "As I say, I am sorry."

And with that, he and his colleagues left the room. I looked at my gaffer.

"How much?" was all he said.

"No idea, at the moment. Haven't reconciled it yet. I will do it now."

Including the bed and breakfast costs, the lunches, dinners, and finally the huge bar tab, our esteemed, but fake, Lord had racked up the grand total of £1,423.17. The equivalent to nearly £4,000 today. That was some going for four nights. What a way to go too. He could have had a much worse demise.

I know I shouldn't, but I have a sneaky admiration for my Lord Brocklehurst. He wasn't a conman who preyed on little old women, just those of us who embraced the circles we thought he moved in. The ones we wished we were in too. It was a class thing, as old as time, and rather pitiful.

My only sadness is that the Princess Anne story he told us that Sunday evening was not remotely true. Pity.

Chapter Four:

As you know, I loved my Bonnie very much. This amazing and wonderful chocolate-brown retriever was by my side from 1995 until 2006. She saw some amazing things through those huge brown eyes. Lock-ins at the pub where I worked when she was just a pup. The sadness and fear of her owner through the abusive relationship with Susan, her dog-nap rescue, the love and adulation from Dawn for the last few years of her life, and then, finally, the added bonus of getting to know and play with my baby daughter, Charlotte.

For all of us who embrace pets, I am sure that you will agree that they become part of the family, although some, like lizards, hamsters, guinea pigs, and even rabbits that I have had the pleasure of having from time to time, do not. I class them as kids' playthings. We adults can count on cats and dogs to be that enduring part of our lives and, as such, they are allowed into the family hierarchy and memories forever.

Bonnie's health had been deteriorating for a few weeks, as the summer of 2006 drew to a close. I had recently dealt with the death of my father, which I will come to very soon, but the build-up, and actual day Bonnie went over the Rainbow Bridge, was far more emotional and deeply sadder than anything my dad's passing could offer.

She had begun to suffer fits. They were terrifying to witness, and I wouldn't wish those episodes on anyone. There is nothing you can do to help, apart from trying to make sure they can't harm themselves somehow. The pure fear in her eyes as those spasms occurred was heartbreaking. A look, from her big brown eyes, that said 'please, help me'.

Our wonderful vet, who had come to love our canine over the years, couldn't help us, or her. He referred us to a brain specialist who, after a couple of visits, thought he could give her some medication that would help. She was, though, 11 years old. The average life span of the breed was between 10 and 12 years. She was slap-bang in the middle of that dreaded timescale and the thought that she might have to go through any more of those traumatic episodes, even with the help of new medication, made the decision to say goodbye quite easy in the end.

I hadn't yet read the book Marley and Me, and the film didn't come out until a couple of years after Bonnie died, so I was not as prepared as I could have been when we took her to the vets for the final time. The short journey was fine. She lay quietly in the back of the car, whilst there was silence in the front. Dawn was desperately trying to keep her emotions intact. As usual, I was in stiff upper lip mode, being a man, keeping it all together for the good of the family unit. How ridiculous that sounds, especially if you had witnessed me just half an hour later.

The vet gave her one last hug for himself, which caught me emotionally by surprise, and we all helped Bonnie onto the large examination table. She was very subdued, and I am sure that she knew what was coming, that it was time to leave us, but she definitely didn't want to.
He then advised that he would leave us for five minutes and return to put her to sleep. That was the moment my 'hard man' persona disintegrated. It was Dawn who managed to keep it together as I crumpled onto Bonnie's large warm body and just wept. It was at that point when I

acknowledged what I was about to lose. Christ, it hurt. In a way I hadn't felt before. It was a pain that I don't want to have again but I know that one day, somehow, it will return in a similar guise and I dread it.

We kept talking to her as the injection took effect, reassuring her that everything was going to be all right. That she would be at peace and chasing tennis balls within a few minutes. It was a strange feeling as her eyes closed and she left us for the final time. I imagined what that scenario would be like if she had been a human. Dawn or Mum, for example. Would I appreciate that way of saying goodbye, the highly charged emotion it would bring about, or would I prefer not knowing, finding out that they had died another way? I honestly don't know. I still can't answer that question.

In normal circumstances, your dog gets cremated. It's easier and more practicable and there are not many cemeteries I know of that house our beloved, but departed, canines. As always, for us, it was not as straightforward as it could have been. The thing was, we did have a cemetery. A family one, based up in the Yorkshire Dales, two hours away. It was at the bottom of a field, where mum lived, and could be viewed from her living room window. The pasture had a little wall around it, and a few trees that sheltered the area.

Buried in that sacred place were the family pets, spanning a number of years. I had never actually used the site myself, or seen a ceremony, but then I hadn't had a pet that had died on my watch. At the outset, though, I was determined that Bonnie should be buried there. I likened it to a family tomb even though it was outside and, in reality, just a grazing meadow for some sheep. Dawn thought this was a bad idea. It wasn't the burial bit that worried her. It was the fact that the site was miles away and having a dead dog with me for a while might send me over the edge whilst I was driving. I totally understood her reasoning, but it was no good, the old girl was going 'home'.

The vet was a little surprised when I told him of our plans, but he was generally supportive, with the caveat that they couldn't keep the body and we would have to take her away immediately. This did cause a logistics issue as Bonnie was booked in for late afternoon and, by the time I had travelled to Mum's, it would be dark and any burial ceremony would have to be put on hold until the following morning. The intelligent thing would have been to rearrange the euthanasia appointment for another day, bright and early, so that I could take her straight to the Dales. I didn't think of that though, so we found ourselves with a deceased canine in the back of the car, heading home for the night.

As I still had her, I wanted Bonnie back in the house for one final time. To lay her in front of the fireplace, on the shaggy dark rug she loved so much. It was Dawn who put a stop to that idea, reminding me of what Charlotte might make of it all. She was barely five years old and sort of understood what was happening to her lovely companion, but it was probably a stretch too far to try and explain that rather macabre occurrence.

"Why don't you just become a bloody taxidermist and you can keep her forever?" asked an exasperated Dawn, as we neared home.

You won't be surprised to know that I had looked it up on the internet. Just in case it was actually possible. It was, but not for someone with fat and useless fingers like me. I was, and still am, the ultimate pen pusher.

In the end, the poor girl stayed in my car overnight. I arranged with Mum that I would arrive the following day, mid-morning, and she said that she would have a couple of helpers ready.

The journey over to my old home was the best. I didn't want it to end. Yes, it was sad, but I spent the whole time just talking to Bonnie. I went through our life together. The first time we set eyes on each other, the time she broke her leg when I got her chasing a tennis ball in the nearby car park and a vehicle reversed over her. Our wonderful holidays in the Lakes, Cornwall, and Scotland. Always booked near a river or woodlands, with a fireplace so she could snore away in the afternoons and evenings. Content. I cried a lot, but they were lovely tears, and it was just like a funeral obituary, albeit one conducted along country roads.

On arrival, there were two young lads outside, kitted out in heavy yellow jackets, wellies and hard hats. I wasn't sure why all these safety measures were in place, to be honest. Mum greeted me with a kiss 'the Spanish way' and a comforting hug. The lads then took Bonnie from the back of my car and headed towards the gate. I followed dutifully and suddenly spotted a huge JCB in front of me.

"What's that for?" I asked innocently.

"To bury darling Bonnie," Mum replied. "How else were we going to do it?"

Hence the safety jackets and hard hats.

I hadn't thought of that bit. I just presumed we would carry her down, use a couple of shovels and Bob's your uncle. I suppose, being seven stone plus, she was going to need a deep burial, and Dawn and I had certainly not found it easy getting her in and out of the car. It was still a shock and not a particularly dignifying one at that.

Before I could protest, Bonnie was in the front bucket and the driver was on his way down the hill. I tried to keep up, walking briskly, but the field was very uneven. Out in front, all I could see was my gorgeous pooch bouncing up and down in the loader as the digger trundled along. Once at the bottom of the field, by the tiny wall that separated the cemetery, the young lad stopped the JCB and emptied poor Bonnie out. It was not a pretty sight.

It was too late to change my mind and the digger dug deep into the ground. How the hell he knew where to start is beyond me. There were no gravestones, no markers to advise who, or what, was where. I was just hoping there hadn't been a recent pet demise, as the thought of seeing something dug up by mistake was not worth thinking about. The hole took seconds to complete, and before I knew it, she was scooped back in the bucket, dumped in the hole, and filled in with the fresh soil. The whole thing took no more than five minutes. I think I shouted 'goodbye' at the top of my voice but I'm not sure she would have heard it over the racket the JCB was making.

The lads disappeared and I had a quick cup of tea with Mum. I didn't say much, as I was still in a daze as I stared out of the window, down the field where my beloved girl had been settled forever.

It was not quite the send-off I had envisaged but I am glad she is buried there. It seems fitting that she is back in the area where it all started, where she was born, and where we had first set eyes on each other.

Chapter Five:

'Dad was dead, to begin with. There is no doubt whatever about that.'

I am sure that some of you will recognise this famous quotation. It is the first line from the wonderful Christmas Carol, by Charles Dickens. I have changed the first word of course, but it sums it up nicely for me. In a way, he had always been dead, from the day I was born to the day he died.

He passed away in 2006. I was 39 years old, living with Dawn and had a beautiful 5-year-old daughter, Charlotte. It didn't stir an ounce of emotion in me. Regret maybe, but more from his perspective than mine. It was him who had missed out on so much, not me. For a few months afterwards, I spent too much time trying to work it all out psychologically. It was pointless in the end and a waste of mental energy. It wouldn't change anything and, to be honest, I was more than okay with that.

I was born where Yorkshire folk would call 'down south'. The family moved up to the Dales when I was 8 years old. Hopefully, this made me an honorary Yorkshireman, but they are a tough lot so they might still need some convincing. I had no idea at the time why we moved 'up north', and whilst I subsequently found out when I was much older, it is not important in the grand scheme of things. Funnily enough, it was the best thing that happened to us as a family, excluding Dad of course.

Village life was idyllic. I adored the outside, the vast array of farms, and the people. We were lucky as there were plenty of children the same age as us, so we just played and played. Mostly external, whatever the weather.

Dad was a salesman so he would leave home early and come home late, travelling around the north, selling his employer's wares to whichever business he could convince. I don't think he was very good at it, to be honest, and maybe that was what contributed to his mood. It was always stinkingly bad.

I actually have no idea why he agreed to or wanted to have children. He took no interest in us, whatsoever. I have no memories of anything we did together, and that's not because I was too young to remember. Trust me, it was zilch.

Christmas time was the worst. He hated it, which was a bit unfortunate when he had three excitable offspring, desperate to open their presents. We had to wait for him to get his arse out of bed which would have been okay if the clock had shown 7 am and not 9.30 am, especially when we had been running around since just after 6 am. A tad cruel when you think about it. The odd thing is that my memories have never concentrated on his lack of attentiveness, especially at that magical time of year, and that is down to two people. My mum and grandma. They made up for any lack of love, or fun, from him.

I was 14 when my parents split up. It was a complete shock, but then you don't know what is going on behind the scenes, do you? Well, some of us don't anyway, luckily. My mum shielded us from it all, especially the split, and I will be forever grateful for that. It meant I could just concentrate on holding hands with a girl called Gillian in the village bus shelter.

I do remember the evening he left though, and not for the reasons you would expect. It is not etched on my brain because I was hurt, or upset that I was about to lose him, but more for the reason that it was the same night they finally arrested the Yorkshire Ripper, Peter Sutcliffe. I must stress now that those twin events were coincidental, but as my father loaded his car with a couple of suitcases, I was glued to the TV, watching the news flash. I found this event far more interesting than waving off my old man.

He found himself a flat about three miles away and in the early stages of the separation we would bike over to see him, spend some pretty uninspiring time in his company, and then cycle all the way back. This arrangement didn't last long and as the weeks and months passed, so the trips dwindled. He still didn't take us anywhere, until one day when he offered me and Craig the opportunity to watch England play Australia at Headingly. The Ashes. The pinnacle of test cricket. To say I was excited by this prospect would have been an understatement.

I should have known it was too good to be true. He didn't have a loving bone in his body. The upshot was that he could get his hands on three tickets, but he couldn't afford to pay for all of them, so we would have to pay for our own. Let's just let that sink in for a minute. He was essentially telling his 14-year-old son, who adored cricket, that he needed to stump up the dosh for an expensive ticket when his only income was delivering logs to the locals on a Saturday morning. Thanks, Dad.

I didn't go, of course, and nor did my brother. Craig could have gone as he had the means, having just bagged a full-time job at a local garage, but he showed solidarity with me. We stuck together like we always had. We were one tight family without him, that was for sure. To rub salt into the wounds, the ticket I could, and should, have had was the day Botham whacked his wonderful 149. I watched it on the telly instead of seeing it live. Dad was there. Summed it all up I think.

Before the year was out, he had moved away from the area. He didn't tell us that he was leaving but, by that time, the visits had become sporadic and the contact minimal. It was a blessing all around, to be honest. We just got on with our lives, oblivious to where he was or what he was doing. It was another 'out of sight, out of mind' moment for me. I should have remembered and learnt from that, when I found my own, slightly different, moment all those years later with my son, Peter. Maybe, in some tiny way, I was like my father. Not a comfortable feeling.

Life rolled on for many years, and I had my ups and downs with Louise and Susan before Dawn came along and saved me. Then one day, out of the blue, my sister, Jess, made contact to tell me that she had seen him in the local Spar. She was still living in the same town we all grew up in. She worked locally, knew what was what, so was pretty sure he had only come back recently. Over twenty years he had been gone. No sight nor sound in all that time and then, suddenly, he was back. For a visit, or for good? Jess said she would do some digging, see if anyone knew anything and report back.

Craig lived over in the North West so it had become customary that, if we ever needed a family conference, we would try and meet halfway. This became the Bradford area and usually at one of those Toby Carverys that had suddenly become very popular. Mum would usually be part of those meets but for that one, an update on Dad's movements, we had decided it should just be the three of us. The upshot was that he had moved back into the area. He was living alone, in a village about five miles away and had been there for a couple of years. I just found it bizarre that he had never tried to find any of us, to ask anyone locally where we were, or what we were up to. We discussed whether we should go and see him. Craig and Jess were adamant. Not a chance.

I wasn't as sure as the two of them as I drove back home. Something was dragging me, like a magnet, to get in touch with him, see him, show him pictures of the granddaughter he didn't know he had. Maybe tell him about my sporting exploits, perhaps even the bits of my life that still hurt. I could talk to him as my dad and as a stranger, all at the same time, in an odd sort of way.

I decided to discuss the situation with Dawn and, if she didn't come out with her immortal line, "You're a knob", I would surprise him and knock on his door.

Chapter Six:

Once again, I found myself driving back to the Yorkshire Dales, for reasons that were not just the twice-a-year obligatory visit to my mum. I remembered the dog nap from a few years before and the time when I drove through the carnage of the foot-and-mouth crisis. This time I was on my way to see a man I had not seen for over twenty years. I was still torn with regards my decision to see him, but Dawn was, as always, a good sounding board. She listened, questioned, made one or two sarcastic jokes, but in the end agreed that this needed to be done.

"No regrets," she had said, followed by, "If it were me, I would go."

The address Jess had given me only helped in a vicinity sort of way. The village he was now residing in was a quaint little hamlet, with no shops whatsoever. The houses and cottages were situated far apart, so even though I knew where the village was, finding his abode would be a little harder.

Both Craig and Jess were not particularly happy with my decision and thought it was a bad idea, that it would only end in disappointment for me. They were probably right, but if I didn't try, I would never know. What if the reunion flicked a fatherly switch in him? A new start for us. One that saw him holding, and playing with, his granddaughter or having a beer and a laugh with his son and daughter-in-law. It had to be worth a shot, surely?

As I entered the village, I slowed down to a crawl. I looked to my left and right as the houses came into view, looking for one, Mandarina Cottage. Some of the buildings were easy to identify, with clear plaques on the gates or fronts, but others were so obscure you had to keep getting out of the car to investigate and either eliminate, or confirm, the dwelling you were hunting down. I must have gone through that hushed community three or four times, getting to the end of the village, and turning round in my Ford Mondeo. That was a feat in itself, being a single-track road with, what seemed like, a moat surrounding the whole area.

Finally, as I contemplated giving up and going home, I spotted a small cottage set back from the main thoroughfare. I must have missed it as I didn't recognise it from my elimination strategy. I drove slowly up the unkempt driveway and parked behind an old blue estate car. I could see a sign on the front of the house, but it was partially covered by the out-of-control ivy clambering all over the brick. I could make out the letters Man... ari.... ge. Although I was not a crossword wizard, even I deduced this must be the one. I gulped and could suddenly feel the sweat starting to fizz on my forehead. I got out of the car, walked slowly to the battered old front door and gave it a forceful knock.

The lock turned slowly from the inside and the door creaked open.

"Hello, Dad," I said, matter-of-factly.

"Good God. Craig," he replied, staring at me through thick reading glasses, his eyes looking ridiculously huge through them.

"Not quite," I uttered wearily. "I'm the other one."

To be fair, you couldn't blame him. I suppose it was a 50/50 call and as Craig was the eldest it was probably the first name that popped into his head. Let us all just celebrate the fact that he remembered any of our names, shall we?

Dad invited me inside and I followed him through the hallway and into the lounge. The only way I can describe what I saw next was heartbreaking. There was a large TV in the corner, nestled on an old and dust-riddled cabinet. A battered old dark maroon chair, that looked like it had escaped from a sofa set, took pride of place in the small room, right in front of the television. A small wooden table was to the right, with just the one, lonely, dining room chair. Opposite it was a traditional dresser with ornaments and a desktop that held a white telephone, with the biggest black numbers I had ever seen, alongside an A4 pad and ballpoint pen. Finally, there was the carpet. It was dark red and cream, worn to within an inch of its life, and covered in, what looked like, numerous dog hairs.

"Do you have a dog?" I asked, trying to break the awkward silence.

"He died about a year ago. He was eleven, so I was expecting it to be fair. He was called Monty. He was a great dog. You?"

"Yes, I do. Bonnie's her name. Lovely dark brown retriever. She is eleven too, so I expect the worse soon."

The thing that struck me, and you are probably ahead of me on this one, was the realisation that the carpet, full of Monty's hair, was still in place, long after his sad demise. It was a quick confirmation that Dad wasn't looking after the house and probably not himself either. He sat down in his chair and directed me to the only other one in the room. I sat, an arm resting on the cheap wooden table, as we attempted to have a conversation.

It was painful, to be honest. He found it hard to converse, as though he had never talked to another human being before. What I did manage to extract was that he had moved to London all those years ago, had been involved in a life-changing car accident, spent a few months in hospital, and from that incident had met a nurse called Maureen, who cared for him and ultimately became his partner. They had moved to this cottage five years ago, enjoyed the countryside together until Maureen had unfortunately succumbed to the dreaded cancer.

As he took me through his relationship with Maureen, I found that this was the only time he talked coherently, with a passion missing from the rest of his dialogue. I could tell he had loved her very much and deduced that he was now very lost without her, that he didn't care about anything anymore. I wanted to hug him, there and then, tell him he wasn't alone any longer, but I couldn't. It's difficult to explain but, at that point, he still felt like a stranger to me. Yes, he was my dad and I felt sorry for him, a child's burning urge to help but, at the same time, I felt detached. A little voice telling me not to get drawn into his plight. It was a mental tug of war at that precise moment.

I showed him some pictures of Dawn and Charlotte, and he was polite and complimentary. I produced more of me, pictures of his other son, Craig, followed by many photos of his daughter, Jess. He continued to look at them, with little comment. To be honest, I desperately needed more than just politeness. I craved emotion from him, maybe a flicker of contrition, but, most importantly, a desire to want to know more, a hint that he wanted to be involved with his estranged children and newly-presented wider family. I got absolutely nothing.

We continued to have a rather stilted conversation, but my thoughts had moved on. The movie in my mind, which had him bouncing his granddaughter on his knee, completely trashed. It was never going to happen. He didn't have to say it, that he still had no interest in any of us, but it was etched plainly on his weary expression. Please, I thought, one final time, show some bloody emotion, but I knew it would never be forthcoming. Craig and Jess were right. It had ended in disappointment once again.

As I got up and prepared to leave, I still couldn't let it go forever.

"Look, Dad. If you ever just want to have a chat, ring me. Anytime. I will leave you my number if you like?"

He looked at me, his expression was still unreadable.

"Yes, okay. That would be nice. Write it down on the pad, would you?"

I walked over to the dresser and started to write my number down. I spotted the giant numbers again on his phone, so I scribbled out what I had written and replaced it with the biggest numbers I could, so he would be able to read it. No excuses.

"There you go. It's right there," I said, pointing at the pad. "Anytime, okay. Promise?"

"Yes, of course. Thanks."

As I exited and made my way to the car, I turned around. He was standing in the arch of the front door.

"Take care, Dad. See you soon," I said, genuinely.

"Thanks. Drive safely."

And with that, he gave a wave and shut the door.

I sat in my car and waited for a couple of minutes, hoping he might come to the window, give me another little wave, but he didn't, of course. I reversed out of the drive and started to drive down the country lane. I had driven for less than a mile when I had the urge to stop. I pulled over, into a rare passing place, and rested my head against the steering wheel. The tears came as I knew they would, a flood that was unstoppable for a couple of minutes.

I never saw my dad again.

Chapter Seven:

You might be relieved to know that, on returning home from my unsuccessful attempt at reconciliation, I didn't spend my days or nights, waiting by the phone. In fact, by the time I had arrived, with a welcoming hug from Dawn, my emotions were intact, and I had, as near as dammit it, forgotten all about it. I was pretty good at that. An expert in my chosen field of blocking out memories and feelings that were harmful to me. For the next few years, once again, I just got on with my life until, one fateful day, when I got the call that, to be honest, I was not dreading.

It was Craig who rang with the news that Dad had passed away. Even in that most simple of scenarios, it was not a straightforward notification. For starters, he had been dead for at least three days before we found out, which was due to the police and council trying to find out if he had any next of kin. His neighbours didn't know of any but had a vague recollection that he had at one time lived in the nearby town and it might be worth asking there.

There was nothing in the cottage to help them with their investigations. Not a great surprise, having been there myself. No pictures on the wall, no correspondence, and no memories to help the poor buggers pass on this particular deceased problem. I presume they never found my giant telephone number that I had written down a few years before. Probably went in the bin before I had hit the main road.

The council, after making enquiries, found my sister Jess, who in turn gave them a contact for his son, and heir, Craig. And so, finally, after a few days, all his children had been informed. I am sure the council gave a huge sigh of relief, but they shouldn't have been so hasty, in hindsight.

Craig took me through where we were, in terms of process, and what needed to be done. There were two main details that needed addressing. Firstly, there was the cottage. Did we, as his children, want to sort the contents, keep what we wanted, and organise the disposal of everything else? Craig advised that he had already said yes to that one.

"No way I wanted to miss out on that opportunity. A chance to go through his things, his documents. We might find some clues that will help us understand who he was and what he had been up to for all those years."

He sounded a bit over-excited, to be honest, but he was a policeman after all.

The second main consideration was the burial and funeral. The council wanted to hand our father over to us so that we could arrange and organise the send-off. It was that part that Craig had stalled them on and wanted my input.

"Jess and I think we shouldn't get involved."

"What do you mean by involved?" I asked, confused.

"As in," he continued, "we don't think we should get involved with his funeral. Let the council do it. Think of the cost. If he has bugger-all in assets, we will be left with the bill. Why should we pay for it?"

It was a valid point but one hell of an apathetic stance to take, even for a specimen as cold-hearted as our dad. I just had this vision that the council's job, when disposing of a body, would only be in extreme circumstances, when no next-of-kin were found and, as such, they had no choice. Not so apparently. We could just say no, you do it. It made me feel uncomfortable. Not for long though. Not when a volcano of Dad's selfish behaviour started to rush to the front of my mind again. Craig was right, and however harsh this may sound, he didn't deserve our love and care in death. We never got an ounce in life.

We informed the council that we were happy for them to make the arrangements for his funeral. They, in turn, advised us that this would be a simple, short cremation with no readings, and just a brief blessing before they set him on fire. I made that last bit up, but you get the idea. Quick, cheap and on to the next one. We confirmed that we were content with this arrangement. God knows what they thought of us. 'Callous bastards' would probably have been the sentiment around their office. We never told them the reasons for this family decision. Maybe we should have.

The main task, therefore, was to empty the cottage. Craig, Jess and I all decided to go together and have a good old snoop. Hopefully, we joked, we might find a will leaving us half a million each but the reality was we might, if we are really lucky, find an old fiver down the back of a chair. As we entered the property, I couldn't help a flood of memories recurring. Just two short years ago, I was there. One last go at reconciliation.

A tinge of sadness came over me as we entered the lounge. The room hadn't changed one iota. Everything was as I remembered, all apart from my phone number. The A4 pad was still there, but blank. If I needed a reminder that I wasn't being a cold-hearted bugger, that helped. Craig took charge as we stood in the middle of the room.

"Right. Jess, you start upstairs. Take your time and don't forget to look in places you normally wouldn't."

His voice was different. Authoritative. A policeman's voice. It was quite reassuring, but also bloody daft.

"This isn't a crime scene, Craig," I said, laughing. "Let's just explore, all together."

Craig smiled apologetically and headed towards the dresser. I spotted him taking some gloves out of his pocket. Latex type, from what I could ascertain. He was snapping them onto his hands, with his back to me.

"What the hell are you doing?" I asked.

"What do you mean?" he answered, turning around.

"The gloves?"

"Oh, I see. Just thought it would help me concentrate that's all."

I looked at him, then at Jess, and we all burst out laughing. It certainly released any tension there might have been.

"I feel sorry for your missus then," I said, still laughing, "if you have to wear them every time you have to concentrate."

"You're funny," he smiled, as he started to open the drawers. "I always leave them in the car anyway."

We got to work. The dresser, that Craig was in control of, was a mass of papers and he had brought them all out and dumped them on the table. I was mesmerised as he started to leaf through them at some speed. It was like watching a bank clerk counting a wad of ten-pound notes, but with A4-size documents. It was very impressive.

He decided to separate them into piles for relevance. Bank statements, bills, life insurance and possibly a will. With regards to the last two, we never found the former, but we did find the latter. There was brief excitement when Craig announced he thought Dad had £50,000 in his current account but, with a swish of his fingers, that was revised down to £3.11. We did deduce, though, that this £50,000 was, in fact, a result of the inheritance his beloved Maureen had left him. Christ knows what state he would have been in without that.

Meanwhile, I was looking through the TV cabinet, perusing the DVDs, when I turned around to say something with regards his choice of movies. I spotted a brown briefcase in front of his favourite, and only, chair. It was tight against the bottom, meaning that a pair of legs would have to hang over it before any feet touched the floor. I hadn't seen it on my only visit but then the way it was facing I wouldn't have picked up on it. I shuffled across and rubbed my sleeve on the top to remove a layer of dust.

It was one of those old-fashioned combination cases that had numbers for locks. I clicked the latches, hoping that he had not set any security. He hadn't, thankfully, and the case opened. The main part, inside, was empty, but as there were a few pockets and zips, I thought I shouldn't leave any stone unturned, as per Craig's instructions. Eliminate any clues, so to speak. It was when I unzipped the last pouch that the bafflement arrived and has stayed with me ever since.

Inside was a small photograph. Just the one. I pulled it out and sat back, leaning against the cabinet. I stared and stared. At us. The picture was of me, Craig, and Jess as children, sat on the sofa from the first home we lived in, all those years ago, in the Yorkshire Dales. We were happy and smiling broadly, with our arms around each other. I hazarded a guess that I was about 8 years old. I wouldn't say it changed everything, mentally, but it was all a bit left-field, to be honest. It was a tad hard to get my head around this precious find. It still is, to this day.

I suppose I will never know if he took the photo out regularly to reminisce, if he looked at it like I was at that precise moment. A look of heartache and emptiness. I hope he did. It would have made me feel a whole lot better, that he had still thought about, and missed, us now and again.

Craig was still fanning his way through the mounds of documentation. I stood up to take the photograph over when we both heard Jess scream loudly. It was like a call to arms. She was upstairs, having done as she was told by our guiding sleuth. We clamoured up the stairs, to where Jess was stood. She was in Dad's bedroom, her hands holding up a double mattress.

"Well, you did say," she laughed, looking at Craig in a triumphant way, "to look in places you normally wouldn't look."

It was some sight. Underneath this old lumpy mass of sponge was a sheet, and on top of that were banknotes. Heaps of them.

"Christ," I said. "This might get those copper juices flowing Craig."

"Indeed," he replied, staring intently, as he snapped a fresh pair of latex gloves on.

Chapter Eight:

The recovery of that startling find wasn't as straightforward as it should have been. I had enthusiastically run downstairs to grab some industrial bin liners, but on my return, the operation to remove the haul had stalled. Craig and Jess were stood, looking upwards.

"What's up?" I asked, before joining them with a gaze towards the ceiling.

I now realised why they had stepped back. Right above Dad's bed was the biggest bulging ceiling you will ever see. A view he must have looked up to, every night. The cracks were so wide I could have put my fingers in them, and they resembled a simpler London underground map. Whilst there was no water dripping from the roof, you could see the damp stains on the tired cream-coloured paint. How on earth it was still up was a mystery.

"You do realise that this hasn't just suddenly appeared," said Craig, as we continued to stare. "That's been building up for a long time."

"I can't believe he actually slept with that above him," I replied, sadly. "Maybe he was secretly hoping it would fall in on him through the night. Put him out of his sad existence."

"Why didn't he tell his landlord?" asked Jess.

"I refer you to my last comment," I said dismissively.

A plan was required. Not a particularly cunning one. Just an agreed strategy that protected our pretty little heads as we made sure we collected the notes from every crook and cranny. Jess had disappeared and I could hear her rummaging around in a separate room, returning with a plastic bowl perched on her bonce.

"Good luck with that," Craig said, sarcastically. "I am no cave rescue expert, but at a guess, I would say that it would be slightly inadequate for the job in hand."

Jess looked deflated. "Hang on," she said triumphantly, looking straight at me. "Have you got a cycle hat in your car?"

"I don't cycle Jess," I replied, with slight exasperation. "Never have, as you can probably tell."

"I know that, but what about Charlotte? She must cycle, that's what I meant."

"She is five, so even if she was a baby Lance Armstrong, her head is that tiny, the thing wouldn't fit on one of my ears, let alone my fat bald head."

An awkward silence descended for a few seconds, broken by Craig's authoritative voice.

"Okay," he said, with clarity. "The best thing we can do is just get on with it. One of you lift the mattress, whilst the other never takes their eyes off the ceiling. I will do the gathering up."

It was like being involved in a sequence of The Crystal Maze, as Craig whizzed in and out to shouts of, "You're fine, the ceiling is okay," or "Keep going, I can hold it," and, finally, "You have missed one, in the right corner."

After about half an hour, Craig sat back against the wall, surrounded by bin liners filled to the top with cash. If we had missed any, it wasn't for the want of trying. We decided to get the heck out of there and scooped up the loot, descending the stairs. We all sat on the floor and started to take the scruffy, and rather damp, twenty-pound notes out of the bags, and onto the worn living room carpet. Something was nagging away at me as we started to put them into £500 piles, a circle forming around us as each stack was completed.

By the time we had completed the task we were looking at £25,000, right in front of our eyes. Mind-boggling, when you think about it. Actually, in the spirit of honesty, it was £24,720 but I will forgive my dad for squandering two hundred and eighty quid somewhere along the way. I should have felt rather pleased with this discovery, but I still had this lingering doubt that something wasn't quite right.

I got up, found my coat and took a wallet out. Thankfully, I had a twenty-pound note, all on its lonesome, and placed it side-by-side with those all laid out on the floor. As I suspected, they were different. They were the same size all right, but the 'twenty' symbol was larger on my crispy new one. I turned them both over and looked for more variants. I didn't need to study long. My note had a face of a gentleman with a huge moustache, whilst our newly-found stash had a completely different person and definitely no facial hair if you excluded his sideburns.

"These are either forgeries or not legal tender," I announced sadly. "I would hazard a guess it's the latter though."

"I agree."

Craig was now studying the different notes closely.

"They are just old notes. Not in circulation anymore at a guess."

"What does that mean though?" asked Jess.

"It means we can't spend it," I replied, gathering up the money and putting it back into the bin liners. "Thought it was too good to be true."

"What do we do with it now then?" Jess asked, shaking her head in disappointment.

"There must be a way of using it or exchanging it somewhere. It's called the black market or something like that, isn't it?"

I looked at Craig for reassurance. He was frowning.

"Probably, yes. But I would rather not get involved for obvious reasons."

"Okay," I said, "let me take it home and give it some thought. I do have one idea."

"What's that then?" Craig replied, warily.

"I will talk to Big Mac. He has fingers in all sorts of pies. He might have an idea how to get rid of it."

Craig nodded.

"His name had crossed my mind too."

Having half a dozen bags full of old banknotes in the boot of my car was actually quite exciting as I trundled up the motorway, ensuring that I kept close to the speed limit. The last thing I needed was to be stopped by a couple of traffic cops, even if my load was legal in a 1990s sort of way. I couldn't decide whether to tell Dawn or wait to see if I could move the money on, confident that I could then tell her that we had just bagged a nice little inheritance. In the end, I thought it made more sense to keep quiet until I had any solid news to tell her.

On arriving home, I put the bags up into the loft. Dawn and Charlotte were out, which was fortunate, as one or two of the drying notes fluttered onto the landing and it was a bit of a scramble from time to time to get hold of them from the draft coming from the open hatch. It was like a scene out of the classic film The Ladykillers, as I tried to hide the loot. Ridiculous in all honesty, as there was nothing criminal about the situation at all. It just felt that way, for some odd reason.

My call to Big Mac was set for the weekend. I made sure that I was on my own as I sat down in the kitchen, all details to hand. He was his usual cheery, booming self as I took him through the events of earlier in the week. I had asked someone I could trust at work for some advice without giving away too much. That work colleague thought, from my descriptions, that the note I was referring to ceased to be legal tender at the end of February 2001. Five years previous. I conveyed this, and some other crucial details, as Big Mac listened intently.

"I can sort it for you," he said when I had finally finished telling him my dilemma. "But this is business, so I want ten per cent. Call it two and a half thousand for ease. When all is done, I will transfer the remainder into your account. No questions asked."

I wasn't sure whether that was a fair price for what I was asking, but as we didn't have a bean at the beginning of the week, the thought of someone else sorting the problem out and me ending up with still the thick end of £7,500 was a no-brainer, so I said yes. We arranged a date for the collection and then I left it in his capable hands.

It was a month later when Big Mac called. It was all done, and I should have the money in my account. Blimey. At that point, Craig and Jess were oblivious to what had just occurred. We had kept in touch and I had advised them that all was in hand, that it had cost us a small share, but was worth it to get the problem sorted without any headaches. They were all on board and in agreement.

"Thanks," I said to Big Mac. "Huge weight off me, I can tell you. I know you won't want to say how you did it, no questions asked and all that, but there wasn't any criminality involved, was there?"

"Of course not," he boomed. "What do you take me for?"

"Sorry. Just still slightly worried, that's all."

"Don't be. I just did what anybody would do. Even you, if you had thought about it."

"I don't understand. What could I have done about it?"

"Just walked into a bank and exchanged it," he thundered. A huge laugh blasted its way down the phone. "You can't spend it in a shop, but you can still bank it as long as you can prove your identity."

His deep laugh continued as his remarks began to sink in.

"You're telling me that I could have just walked into a bank myself? Deposited it, with no questions asked?"

"Yep."

"But I gave you two and a half grand."

My voice was getting higher and louder.

"That's your own fault, not mine. You asked me to get rid of it. You should have done your homework and not had such a guilty complex. All old banknotes can be exchanged."

You probably knew all of this. I didn't. It hadn't even crossed my mind. I honestly just thought the whole lot was defunct. All that wasted energy, thinking that we were doing something wrong. Scared of God knows what. That's a guilty mind if ever there was one.

I didn't tell Craig and Jess at the time; I was far too embarrassed. I am sure they must have realised sometime later, in the years since, but it was never mentioned.

Let's be honest, they were just as dim as I was.

Chapter Nine:

My acute embarrassment with the family heist debacle didn't last long. I soon turned my attention to what I should do with this new-found wealth. It would have been nice if I had been luckier and had a normal and loving relationship with my dad, as I would probably have spent it on some fancy memorial or visited a holiday destination we had enjoyed together. Instead, I found myself measuring up for a new kitchen.

It was Dawn who stopped me in my tracks and queried my decision. As always, she was the more mature one in our relationship. She always thought things through in more detail. I was deep in concentration, tape measure spread across the floor, leaning on the kitchen table and scribbling down measurements, as she approached quietly, putting her arms around me from behind.

"Have you read his will?" she asked in a gentle, affectionate voice.

"I have had a quick glance," I replied, ensuring that I had finished writing the length of the kitchen floor on my infant-style plan. "Why do you ask?"

"He may have said where he wanted his estate to go."

"That's going to the scrapyard, D. It's worthless."

"No, you knob," she laughed. "Not his bloody car. His E-S-T-A-T-E."

She said the last word slowly like she was spelling it out to Charlotte.

"What he wanted to leave, his assets and stuff, and to whom. Have you looked?"

I turned around and faced her, smiling in a condescending way.

"He didn't have a pot to piss in, did he? What's the point in reading it?"

"But he did though, didn't he?" she said, quite forcefully. "Nearly twenty-five thousand pounds in the end. I know it's none of my business but before you go ahead and spend it, just stop and give it some thought. Read it please."

Talk about a sudden emotional twinge. I sat down as Dawn gave me a peck on the cheek and went into the back garden. Okay, I thought to myself, let's think about this rationally. He had no immediate family bar us. He had nothing in his bank account. No Antique Roadshow paintings that Michael Aspel could make us faint with, in some country garden. Technically, he didn't have one asset, apart from the battered old estate car that needed to go to the knacker's yard. However, we had found a rather large amount of old money under his bed. Did that count? What do you think? Of course, it did.

Craig had Dad's last will and testament. I had no idea if he had read it or not but when I rang and asked him for a copy, he confirmed that he hadn't touched it since we ransacked the place and that he would post the original as he had no interest in what it said.

Out of all of us, I think Craig was hit hardest by Dad's absence, especially immediately after he left. Not because of any emotional loss as he, like me and Jess, didn't miss what we had never had. We got all the love and support we needed from Mum, each other, and Grandma. It was more of a financial burden for Craig.

He was 17, had left school and got himself a nice job at a local garage selling Land Rovers when the split came. As such, he ended up helping and supporting the family. School shoes for me. A ballet dress for Jess. Things that Mum couldn't afford anymore. Instead of spending his well-earned wages on wine and women, he spent them on me. It was no wonder that he couldn't forgive and had no interest in the written contents of the will of someone he disliked very much.

The plain brown envelope, bearing my dad's last wishes, arrived a few days later. I was due at work, so I left it on the kitchen worktop. I needed more time than a quick glance just in case there was anything important in it. I had noticed that it was thicker than I had expected and as the working day continued so my interest in its contents deepened. How could there be so much information for someone who had jack shit?

That evening, we put Charlotte to bed and settled down in the living room. Dawn was lying full length on the sofa, her legs across mine as I sat at the end. I started to read the will, skimming through the jargon and solicitor's wording, trying to find the juicy bits, if any.

It was on the third page that I landed on the first of two instructions that became important in the following days.

The first one was his wish to be cremated. That bit was all in hand, thanks to the local council, but there was a little more detail than that. His final wishes were to have his ashes scattered at a certain point, described in great detail, on a particular moor in the Yorkshire Dales. Odd, I thought, but I decided to come back to that part.

The second one, and even more important, was the page that dealt with his assets and beneficiaries. It was that part which made me sit bolt upright, waking Dawn from her light sleep. I can't remember the exact wording, but it went something like this.

'I give my Estate absolutely to the following. Maureen O'Brien. If Maureen O'Brien dies in my lifetime my residuary estate shall be passed to the beneficiaries named in this subclause.'

That all meant sense as Maureen was his loving partner. It wasn't long before I got to the all-important subclause.

'If there are surviving beneficiaries, then my residuary shall be given to; A) Any grandchildren that are, at the time of my death.'

That was it. No further written word on his wishes for his estate or reasoning. Primarily, anything available was to be given to his grandchildren. Persons he didn't know existed. Had never met. Whilst he had found out about Charlotte when I had visited him two years prior, I can guarantee that the will was much older than that. It was bizarre. 'Why?' was all I could say to myself, as I sat back on the sofa letting out a deep sigh.

"What does it say?" asked Dawn, sleepily.

"I just don't get it," I replied, confused. "He has requested anything, and everything, should go to his grandchildren. So, Charlotte I suppose."

At that moment, I was the only one who had any children. Craig was, as he kept telling me, practising hard, and Jess was recently out of a long-term relationship, with no children involved.

"And Peter, of course," Dawn suddenly announced. "You shouldn't forget him. He is your dad's grandchild too if you are going to be true to his wishes."

She was right, as always. If I was, and it was a big if, be true to my father's requirements, then, in reality, Peter and Charlotte should each get half of the mattress money that I had earmarked for the kitchen. Even more importantly, and if I could find any moral compass, then they should also get the share currently burning a hole in Craig and Jess's accounts. What a mess.

I stayed up long into the night. Dawn listened to my ramblings for a while but, in the end, had to give up for some well-needed sleep. There were a couple of things that were bothering me. One was whether I should do the right thing, which would mean discussing it with Craig and Jess, gathering their thoughts, and deciding as a family. The other was more disturbing and that was whether, somehow, Dad had known about Peter and that was the reason he had written the subclause in that specific way. That would mean he knew more about me than I had realised. It was a spine-tingling thought, I can tell you.

I would never know, of course, unless Louise fessed up to being in contact with him over the years, but that was pretty far-fetched, even for my imagination. I decided I would ring her anyway, just in case. Meanwhile, I called a family summit at our usual haunt on the outskirts of Bradford.

Craig and Jess read the will as we tucked into a rather sad-looking carvery. I sat quietly, awaiting their comments, genuinely comfortable with whatever they would decide, although the feelings I had, that we should do the right thing, were getting stronger by the minute. I didn't believe in the afterlife, that there was something that happens to us after we die, in a spiritual way. My thought process was that we got eaten by worms, or burnt within seconds, and that was that. His wishes, though, had freaked me out. I had dreamt, the night before, that he was sat on a bench, up in heaven, seeing if I was going to do the right thing and tell my brother and sister about Peter. Willing me to come clean.

This, in my head, was what it had become about. Truth and honesty. A reminder to me not to make the same mistakes as he had. Probably a load of old twaddle, but it was too late, as it was firmly implanted in my thinking. Craig was first to speak.

"Interesting," he said, as he finished reading, chomping the last, weary, roast potato on his plate. "But, and don't take this the wrong way, I don't see what you are getting at unless you are just saying that Charlotte should have the money. If it is, just say it."

Jess interjected. "I don't mind if you want to do as it states and let her have it. I'm happy to give it back."

"I do," snapped Craig.

"It's a bit more complicated than that," I began. "All a bit odd. I think it's a bit of a test. For me. Maybe for all of us. I think he knew, you see. I don't know for sure."

"What are you babbling on about?" Craig interrupted. "He knew what? What kind of test?"

"The thing is that Charlotte isn't his only grandchild. He has another one."

There was silence and a change of expression in both of them. They stared at me intently, knowing that it wasn't either of them so...

"I have a son. He's called Peter. Hopefully after Beardsley but I haven't found that bit out yet, to be honest. Be good if it was though. Nice tribute."

"Stop," Craig interrupted again. "I got lost when you started going on about Peter Beardsley. Start again. You have another child and he's called Peter. Have I got that bit right?"

"Yep. Spot on."

I then just let it all out. How he came to be, a bit about Louise, that he was living back in London with her, and he was 16. Oh, and he hadn't a clue who I was. At first, there was a bit of anger that I hadn't told them sooner, but this thawed when they understood that I had only known for four years myself.

"So, I think he knew somehow. Don't ask me how and why," I summed up. "And that he wants me to do the right thing. Like he didn't, through his children's lives."

Craig took a sip from his glass of shandy.

"I get it. I think you are thinking way too deeply about all the circumstances, but I do get it, why you think we should do this. The flip side is that I think he will be pissing himself laughing at me ... at all of us. I imagine. Like he did when he cleared off."

As a counterargument, it was pretty powerful.

"But," he concluded, "I can do without it. We never expected to have it, and if it helps your lad, for something or other, then I'm happy to let him have it."

Jess nodded. That was my family in a nutshell. Looking after each other. We had done it all our lives.

"Thank you," I said. "I know it doesn't make any sense, but I think I might sleep easier for the rest of my life."

Back home, I gave Dawn the details of our summit. I could tell she was pleased that I was doing the right thing, for both of them. I did sneakily suggest that Charlotte's half could still be invested in a new kitchen and when she was older I would show her what her investment had been used for. I could demonstrate how it had made life easier, not just for her, but for her mum and dad too. You will know, by now, what her reply was.

A few weeks later, I called Louise to give her the news. She was genuinely shocked and delighted that a man she had never met, had never known, had left some money in that way for Peter. I had stopped myself asking the question that had been eating away at me but, at the last minute, I couldn't resist. I just had to ask, however daft it might sound.

"You never met him then? Never knew him at all. Somewhere your paths might have crossed?"

I knew it sounded ridiculous.

There was a pause down the line. A tad too long for my liking.

"No … I would have told you … I don't think so … but … I wonder … it can't be …"

"It can't be what?" I interrupted urgently.

"WHAT CAN'T IT BE?" I asked again, louder.

"I did look after a man, years and years ago, who had been in a car accident. He said he was originally from Yorkshire and I remember saying I had a boyfriend from there. He asked me how old this lad was, what he did, what he looked like, that sort of thing, but he was just passing the time, interested in small talk whilst he lay recovering, as you do when you are bored."

"Go on," I said, beginning to shake, the phone somehow still in my hand.

"I was heavily pregnant when this man was there. He asked me if the baby I was having was from this lad and I said it was, but he mustn't tell anyone. That it was a secret. 'Mum's the word' we would both say and touch our noses with our fingers. We were just bantering. I remember saying it was funny that he had the same surname. I started to call him Grandad which made him laugh. It can't have been him though. Just a daft coincidence."

She was probably right but then a name suddenly remerged in my memory. It was screaming at me to say it out loud.

"You didn't know a Maureen O'Brien, did you? Another nurse that would have been there at the same time?"

There was another long pause.

"Yes, of course," Louise answered, rather surprised by the question. "She was my boss. How on earth do you know her?"

How do you process that sort of information? That your dad, who had never stayed in touch, lay in a hospital bed and deduced, or guessed, that his son was about to become a father. He then decided to leave whatever assets he may have, at the time of his death, to a grandchild he would probably never meet. The honest answer is, I couldn't. I would just have to live with it.

What it did change, for me, was the certainty that I would carry out the other wish he had requested in the will. He had asked for his ashes to be scattered in a particular place and nothing was going to stop me from carrying out his final plea.

Chapter Ten:

The council sporadically kept in touch with us with regards to the funeral arrangements. I say arrangements in the loosest sense of the word, as they just informed us of the venue and the time of cremation. I am not being critical. It was our decision to wash our hands, and pass him over to them, but I was getting a few twinges of regret. The previous few days had thrown up one or two curveballs but it was too late by then. We just had to go along with whatever was planned.

My pangs of guilt, following the strange circumstances surrounding the beneficiaries of his will, made me think of a plan to properly send him on his way. Whilst I couldn't do anything to influence the actual funeral, I could arrange other things to say a proper goodbye. The scattering of his ashes was the main one, but I also fancied arranging a farewell family dinner in his honour.

To be honest, Craig and Jess were getting exasperated with my constant phone calls. My suggestions that we should do this, or that, to give our dad a fitting tribute. Whilst they totally understood that my whole perception had changed, and they agreed that the will's contents were all a bit odd and unexplainable, they still made sure they kept reminding me of the real dad, the one in life who had abandoned us, and who I had even given one last chance just a couple of years before. Those conversations did jolt me back to reality, but not for long. I had got to the stage that I was fearful if I didn't follow through with all his instructions, that something terrible would happen to me, or my family.

I still don't understand why I felt that way. I had never been religious, even though I had been that humiliated head choir boy nearly thirty years ago. I wasn't spiritual in any way, didn't believe in life after death, clairvoyants, or hypnosis for that matter. I had experienced the last two, the first to try and get in touch with my grandma, the second to help me give up smoking. Neither worked. It was Dawn who suggested that I should maybe try again, the clairvoyant I mean, that this time it might be helpful. I suppose my thought process was that I had nothing to lose, so the idea began to gain traction.

That was in the days before Facebook had exploded so, in fairness, those mediums did have a tad more guesswork to do than these days, Today, all they have to do is just pop your name into Google and Bob's your uncle. They know the whole damn lot. Back then, I was a cynical so and so. Dawn said I needed to open my mind, clear it of all negative and distrustful thoughts, that I might gain something if I wasn't such a knob. She had a point.

Dawn had found a lady based in Leeds. She had come highly recommended by some of her close friends and also the dance teacher at Charlotte's school. I'm not sure that these endorsements were of high calibre but with nothing to lose and to shut my beloved partner up, I made an appointment.

The lady was called Miranda or Gypsy Miranda, as I nicknamed her, which didn't go down well at home. Dawn's death stares were not to be scoffed at, and my blasé approach to my forthcoming date with destiny resulted in her ignoring me for vast periods. I was trying to imagine being open and not cynical, but even if she was any good at what she did, how the hell would I know? I had no memories to draw on as the man I wanted to get in touch with wasn't there for the majority of my life. I started to feel sorry for the medium as she was going to have one hell of a struggle finding something to connect us. If the whole thing was real.

The reading occurred at our agreed date and time and I found myself in a small dining room. It was traditionally set out with carpets and furniture from another era. It reminded me of my grandma's flat and I felt strangely comforted. There was no crystal ball on the table which was disappointing and Miranda was dressed in jeans and a light jumper that had the slogan 'There is no greater wealth in this world than peace of mind' which made me feel uneasy, for some reason.

We did the introductions and sat opposite each other. She had a lovely soothing voice, kind and thoughtful, and she asked me some general questions followed by who I wanted to speak with from the spirit world. I was tempted to say David Bowie, so that I could apologise for trashing his music when he was alive, but I resisted being an arse and went with the traditional. My dad, please.

The early part of the reading was rather bland. She mentioned a few names that I didn't recognise, a few places and, to be honest, I was getting a bit frustrated but also triumphant that this, as I thought, was a load of old baloney. Boredom was setting in when she suddenly piqued my interest.

"I can see a milk float. Someone seems to be upset. A little boy or girl. They are crying. Your dad says that he wasn't angry. Just scared. He says he is sorry he hurt you."

I leant forward, with my elbows propping me up on the table. Miranda was looking at me, waiting to see if I would respond. You won't believe how I fought that moment. How I desperately didn't want to say anything, that it would be an admission of defeat, that Miranda had won. How utterly bizarre and self-defeating was that? I pulled myself together and for the first time let my mind open, to go with the flow.

"Tell him that it's all right. Tell him that I understand now, being a dad myself."

I could feel the tears gently escaping as my memory transported me, way back, to a time when I was 6 years old and I jumped onto the milk float that delivered to our house and the surrounding area. The milkman had no idea, for a while, that I was hiding at the back as he delivered through the streets. I have no idea why I did it, fun I suppose, but when I was found and returned home my dad gave me the belt, painfully, on my young bottom.

"I can see Big Ben."

Miranda brought me out of my painful memory.

"And a hospital. He is happy that he was right."

"I don't understand, sorry."

"No," she said, angrily. "He is saying that I am not listening. Tell me again then," she said, looking to her right, as though someone was stood beside her. "Ah, yes okay. He is saying you did the right thing. That he was a good detective."

"He was a carpet salesman and wasn't even in the police," I answered sarcastically. "His other son is though. He had a habit of making that mistake, mixing us up."

She ignored me.

"I can see Big Ben again, the same hospital. A young man is stood outside. He looks very proud. Very handsome in his school uniform."

She looks at me, quizzically.

Even though I had a feeling where it was going, that I had an idea what she, or my dad, was trying to say, I had, for some reason, put my sceptical hard hat back on. I was thinking, go on, give me more, give me absolute proof you are talking about him.

"For some reason, I can see a football stadium."

Miranda was now in full flow.

"There is a sign. St. Jim? No, St. James. He is getting a bit agitated with me again, saying I'm not listening. I can see colours, black and white. There is a number 6. No, a number 9. He is shouting at me again."

"Okay," I said calmly, "that's enough. Christ, talk about making me want to engage."

Miranda smiled.

"Does any of this mean anything to you?"

"He is talking about my son. That I have never known. Not my fault, I hasten to add. He's 16 now and lives in London with his mum, who is a nurse. She looks like Peter Beardsley who wore the number 9 shirt, in black and white colours, for a team called Newcastle who play at St. James Park. She looked after Dad when he was recovering from an accident. I think that covers it."

"Ah, I see," she said in her soothing voice. "He is smiling now, but he just keeps saying, sorry."

"So he should. Tell him apology not accepted, I'm afraid."

"He is showing me a piece of paper. Waving it at me. I can't see it properly."

She paused and concentrated for a few seconds.

"Numbers, I can see large numbers on it. He is shouting again. Sorry, he is saying. Just the word, sorry."

My phone number. The one I left at his cottage a couple of years before. That was enough for me. I didn't need anything else. I was done, emotionally spent. Thankfully, there was nothing much more that came after those rather draining communications. Miranda, looking tired, bid me farewell, her calm voice soothing me as we said our goodbyes.

"I hope this has helped and whatever he said today can heal some wounds," she said, as I left.

I hoped so as well, but there were still too many negative memories, an emptiness spanning over 25 years, that no number of apologies would suffice. At least he had tried, at last. Just a tad too late if truth be told.

Today, I can proudly state that I do believe in all things afterlife and spiritual. I know that when I pass away, I will go somewhere better, that I will be okay, watching over those I love and giving silent guidance. I won't just be in a casket, burning away for a few minutes, or just lying there, being nibbled underground by a family of worms.

For all his faults, Dad has enabled me to feel this way. Possibly the best gift he could have ever given me, to be honest. I feel more at ease with myself now, knowing that one day, it will be my turn to leave this world.

Chapter Eleven:

The day of my dad's funeral was a strange one, in many ways. There were no last-minute preparations. We had not informed anyone, as there wasn't anyone to tell. Dawn decided to stay at home and have a normal day with Charlotte. That made sense as we hadn't mentioned anything to her, being so young, and Dawn didn't have a clue who he was anyway. She had offered to come, to be a support and shoulder to cry on if needed, but the reality was that I didn't need it.

Craig, Jess and I had arranged to meet at a café just outside the town where he was being cremated. It was a dull day, with big dark clouds moving at great speed over the hills of the beautiful Dales. It wasn't cold but the breeze did warrant a jacket and trousers. Black, of course. It's one of those outfits we all have. Just in case. The obligatory black tie, shirt, or dress somewhere in the wardrobe. Right at the back, a bit fusty, knowing we might need it sometime. Hoping we won't. Always there though, waiting patiently.

We sat outside on uncomfortable metal chairs that seemed to have different measurements for each leg. Why do most cafés have those useless seats? The ones where you are constantly wobbling away, as you chat. Is it mandatory? The coffees were the size of a breakfast bowl but mostly absent of caffeine, filled to the brim with frothy hot milk. We tried to reminisce, but we found it hard-going. I told them about Miranda, the milk float, and the Peter Beardsley reference. They were intrigued as I regaled them both with the tale, and they sat open-mouthed when I got to the juicy bits.

"Bizarre," said Craig. "There's something in this afterlife, that's for sure. I still can't help feeling sceptical about it all though. I suppose you have to go yourself to really believe."

"You should," I answered. "You never know, it might help with how you feel."

"I don't think so. Might be a world first though. Spirit and entity scrap, with the clairvoyant as referee."

We managed to recollect a couple of memories as we waited for our time slot. We recalled the time that Dad had left the handbrake off in his company car by mistake and it had subsequently rolled down the driveway and into the side of the house. The kitchen window faced the driveway and, apparently, his face was a picture as he witnessed, in slow motion, the grill and headlights heading towards him.

Craig stated that he only had one happy memory and that was when we went on holiday in 1971. He was, he recalled, about 8 years old and we were still living in the south. He remembered a drive up to the Lake District, where we were going on holiday for the week. Jess and I shook our heads, no recollection whatsoever. I suppose I would have been four at the time, and my sister only one year old. A bit young to recognise anything at that age. Craig was convinced that it was that trip that made Dad fall in love with the Yorkshire Dales, as we had stopped off for a break, at the town we ended up living in, before going on our merry way.

"There's a song," he mused, "that, when it comes on the radio, transports me straight back to that journey. The three of us sat in the back, me singing along as Dad was driving."

Craig looked up into the hills, the clouds still threatening. He was lost in thought.

He continued, "It has become a bit more common lately with that police drama on TV. The song is played constantly now."

We were listening to him intently, but that last sentence had me and Jess suddenly switching to quiz mode.

"Police drama. What year?" I asked.

"This year. That's what makes it all a bit uncanny, and a bit of a strange coincidence. If you believe in those things of course."

"Must be Life on Mars then," Jess announced, triumphantly. "It's brilliant."

We were back to David Bowie. I wondered whether, even at the age of four, this had, subconsciously, shaped my dislike of the man who called himself Ziggy Stardust. I had though become a connoisseur of the great man's back catalogue in later years, so felt empowered to challenge my brother's memory.

"Life on Mars didn't come out until 1973," I said smugly, wobbling away in my uncomfortable metal chair. "So, you must have your dates mixed up."

Craig looked at me with disdain.

"It was 1971. The song was on the album, Hunky Dory, which came out that year. Dad played the whole cassette constantly. All the way there and back. Life on Mars came out as a single in 1973, so that's when everyone got to know it. It was the song I loved most though and kept asking him to rewind and play it again."

Craig lowered his head. If there were any tears, he was hiding them. It was the first time I had seen any emotion or sadness from him, regarding anything to do with Dad. Good old Bowie had got him there.

I looked at my watch. It had just gone twelve and our slot was for 12.30.

"Come on," I said, using the famous line from the movie Pulp Fiction. "Let's get into character."

The surreal nature of what was about to happen was none more palpable than arriving at the crematorium and an empty car park. I imagined what this would have looked like if he had led a completely different life, with a family and a vast bank of friends. There would have been cars everywhere, a mass of people, mostly in black, silently congregating, a few hugs here and there, lots of handshakes. Instead, it was just the three of us. I felt crestfallen.

We sat on a bench outside the main entrance waiting for our turn. The flowers surrounding the building and pathways were a glorious colour and brightened up the drab and uninviting building in front of us. The clouds were getting darker and moving quickly across the sky. For a brief moment, it reminded me of The Omen.

Suddenly there was a huge roar, as two fighter jets passed straight over the crematorium.

"Right on time," Craig said. "Nice gesture."

The three of us burst out laughing. His quip certainly eased the emotional tension and mixed feelings that were building up inside us all. I looked at my watch again. Ten minutes to showtime. I was getting a bit cold and contemplated getting back in my car to get a quick burst of warmth. I stood up and looked back towards the car park where I saw a convoy of cars coming up the long driveway. I counted at least eight as they parked up alongside our lonely automobiles.

The group of people who got out of their cars were certainly together. A dozen of them, I guessed, heading towards us and the grim building we were about to enter. I was struck by their attire as they all seemed to be dressed in green and I wondered if it was a tribute to the person they had come to pay their respects to. I presumed that they were due in after us, which if so, was going to test their resolve against the elements.

They congregated outside the entrance and we decided to leave our bench and get to the front just in case they intended to push in. That honestly was my thought process at the time. How crass and preposterous was that?

We all stood together, silently, and I then noticed why they were all in green. The majority of them had badges with their name on, with the familiar black and yellow logo of Morrisons above each one. I reckoned that they must have been staff from the local supermarket, come to wave off a former colleague or something similar.

"You must be after us," I said, approaching a middle-aged lady with silver hair and huge earrings that gave me an instant flashback of sitting behind Bet Lynch when I was a young teenager.

"Yes," she replied, "they must be running late. We were due in at 12.30."

"12.30?" I replied, surprised. "I think you must have got muddled up. We are in at 12.30 pm."

"Oh. Hang on. I will check."

She called her colleague over.

"Alice, this man says he is in at 12.30. Are you sure that's the time for us?"

Alice, a large lady, similar in age with dark wispy hair, nodded.

I queried again. This time, directly to Alice. "Who are you saying goodbye to? If you don't mind me asking."

"Alan Wilcox. Who are you here for?"

"Alan Wilcox," I replied, looking at her in a confused state.

"Who are you?" she asked kindly.

"His son," I replied, with a sympathetic smile.

"Oh my God," Alice screamed loudly. "You're his son? I didn't know he had any children."

She gestured to her colleagues to join the two of us, as though she had just come across a new messiah.

"Everyone, I can't believe it, but apparently this is Alan's son."

"He has two more children, apparently," I smiled, genuinely. "Just behind me."

"Oh my God," Alice shouted again. "He had three."

The group gathered around and, for the next few minutes, there were many handshakes and a few awkward hugs. My wish, that there would be lots of people there, had partially come true. It was, though, all a bit bizarre. After some name swapping, I pulled Alice to one side.

"I'm sorry, but I don't understand. What are you all doing here?"

"To say goodbye to your dad, silly," she said, with genuine affection. "He was such a lovely man. We adored taking care of him. Packing his bags, finding his money when he couldn't remember where it was. He was always doing that."

She laughed and I nodded in mutual acknowledgement.

"He was always just so happy. Chatting away and telling jokes."

Alice was animated as she described this complete stranger to me. At that point, it would have been churlish to sit her down, put my hands on her shoulders and tell her to calm the heck down. To take her through my 39 years of pain and sadness just to balance the books, so to speak. So I didn't. Instead, I just listened as she carried on describing this wonderful man I never knew.

"He never said he had any children. Nor did Maureen, God bless her. You must miss your mum too."

"Maureen isn't our mum. I never met her, I'm afraid."

"Oh, sorry."

This revelation seemed to stop Alice in her tracks. I could see that her mind was now visualising everything, the conversations they all had together.

"I just thought ..."

"It's okay," I interrupted. "I would have thought the same."

The doors opened and it was time to go in. The Morrisons team were kind enough to let us go first. Not sure what the funeral director made of it as the three of us entered, dressed immaculately in black, followed by a group in name badges, aprons and tabards.

We sat at the front as the short service was delivered. There was not a flicker of emotion from the three of us, but behind us I could hear a few sniffles, at least one person crying loudly, and as it ended, a universal 'Amen' reverberated around the walls. We certainly didn't feel alone paying our final respects, that's for sure.

Back outside, we continued to have conversations with the supermarket staff. One of them stated what a beautiful service it was. It was not a description I would have used.

Clinical, efficient, and soulless would be nearer the truth. Having said that, it was not as lifeless as it would have been without them.

I managed to catch Alice before she left. I had established that it was their lunch hour which, in a way, made it even more lovely that they had dashed up here to pay their respects. I knew they were conscious of the time.

"Can I ask you something, before you go?"

"Yes, of course you can my love," Alice replied, a sad smile glued to her face.

"It's an odd one actually, but were you on the checkout desk when he came in?"

She nodded. "I was. Always there for him. Saturday morning, usually very early. That was his main shop for the week."

"I don't suppose you remember if he bought pork pies and baked beans whilst he was there? Daft question I know."

Alice laughed out loud.

"Yes, he did, every week, without fail. He always used to say, 'that's Saturday lunch sorted' as I popped them through the till."

"Good to know," I smiled. "I kind of hoped you were going to say that."

I shook her hand but she let go, motioned a 'come here' gesture, and we embraced tightly. It lasted a while, as though I was saying goodbye to an auntie I hadn't seen for many years and one that I wouldn't see again.

We let them disappear in their respective cars and then wandered slowly down the hill to the car park. I smiled to myself. Pork pie and beans. Another memory had suddenly been triggered as I had talked with Alice and her colleagues.

My dad used to take me to the shop on a Saturday morning and buy fresh pork pies and a tin of baked beans. I can't picture how old I might have been, or where it was, but I do remember holding his hand.

"That's Saturday lunch sorted, son," he would say, on our way back.

I kept thinking of this memory as I drove home. It was a reminder, albeit a small one, that once upon a time, there was love, somewhere deep inside him. I wondered why it was never sustained.

I also realised that I wouldn't have had that mental souvenir to cherish if it weren't for Alice and the team from Morrisons.

Thank you, wherever you are now.

Chapter Twelve:

With the cremation over, my thoughts turned to Dad's final wish. Operation Ashes to Ashes was born and put into action. I dug the will out one final time to remind myself of how and where he wanted his ashes scattered. The easy part was the destination. Back to the Yorkshire Dales again. The next piece of the jigsaw was okay too, as it described an area above the town that I grew up in, with a single track. That part, my memory could compute. It was the last request that had me a bit stumped. It described, in great detail, a stretch of moorland that housed a rock, and a specific one at that. Ridge Rock.

The Dales are a vast area, as some of you will know. For those of us lucky enough to have lived there, we have the distinct advantage of getting to know the little nooks and crannies. The back roads, hills, and segments that were named hundreds of years ago but, in most cases, didn't make any sense at all, even at the time.

The problem I faced was that I had never heard of Ridge Rock. I made enquiries, starting with my immediate family, which drew a blank. I moved on to friends like Big Mac, but he too was at a loss at what it was or, more importantly, where it was. They all said the same thing. There was only one rock they knew of and that was the huge bugger that overlooked the whole town, but it wasn't called Ridge.

The local council drew another blank, although they had probably blacklisted my name by now, seeing as they had to do the heavy lifting with regards Dad's disposal. Either they were genuine in their baffled response or they decided I could swing. I am sure it will have been the former.

I trawled through the internet, visited the library, but found no reference to the not-so-famous rock. In the end, I decided that we would just have to go to the area described and, with a bit of luck, stumble on his desired resting home. Not easy, but I was confident it would stand out, that it would find us. The previous week had opened my eyes to many things that could not be explained. I felt I was being guided through the money, the mesmerising clairvoyant Miranda, and finally the team at Morrisons. Of course, I would find that damn rock.

We decided to make a weekend of it, the whole family, including Mum. Up to that point, she had wanted nothing to do with the proceedings. We kept her informed at all stages, but she had no desire to see where he had lived, nor to attend the cremation, but had decided that she wanted to be part of scattering his ashes. I sometimes forget that they were together for over twenty-five years, meeting as teenagers and falling in love at an amateur theatre group. She would have had plenty of memories, plus three wonderful children. There would have been some good times in those corresponding years. I think, in the end, she wanted to say one final goodbye too.

We made the familiar long journey over to the Dales. Dawn had fallen asleep, which was usually the case before we had even got out of the driveway. Bonnie was panting away in the boot, slobbering over the rear windscreen, and finally, there was Charlotte, strapped tightly in her child seat, dressed in pink with a Tweenies top showing her favourite character, Fizz. As a tribute to Dad, and to recreate the memory Craig had described at the crematorium, I played the David Bowie album, Hunky Dory, all the way to Mum's. Particular attention was given to Life on Mars and I tried to teach Charlotte to sing the chorus as we drove along, singing the title line as loud as I could, imploring my daughter to join in. She did manage the odd 'Mars' without the M, and 'Life' without the L, which made me smile.

We had decided to have dinner the evening before, courtesy of a small amount of the mattress money which we kept back for any unforeseen emergencies. This wasn't one of them, but Mum was adamant that if anyone was going to pay for this forthcoming banquet, it was him. One way or another.

The small town didn't have many restaurants in those days. I recall that there was an Italian above a small convenience store, the pubs, of course, and finally, a bistro called Tiny Tim's. It was owned by a local man called Tim, and it was very, very tiny. At a push, I think it housed six tables, but they were so close to each other that you would never have dreamed of taking a date there. Everyone would have known your business by sunrise and even what debauchery you might have planned for the night.

I have no idea why we chose to dine there. I think it was because it was the most expensive, so it was a bit of a 'finger in the air' to our duly departed father. In addition to the three of us, there was Mum, Craig, his wife Lisa, and, finally, Jess. The Magnificent Seven, as Dawn nicknamed us for the evening. Even though we had booked, we seemed to cause all sorts of panic for poor Tiny Tim as he arranged three tables to get us all squeezed in together. I think he could have taken just one more booking for that night. If they were on their own, very thin, and under 5ft tall, that is. As it was, it was just us. Lovely and private.

The dinner was excellent. It might have been a minuscule venue but the food was pretty good, and the service quick and non-intrusive. The wine flowed. Red and white in equal measure. Mum was telling stories of her young life with Dad, then our early lives together. We listened, laughed, and even had the odd sombre tear as the evening progressed. It was past 11 pm, when I summoned the waiter and requested a couple more bottles of wine. One of each coloured grape.

"I'm sorry, Sir, but we have run out."

"I'm sorry?" I replied, incredulously. "You have run out. Totally, or the ones we were drinking?"

"Any wine, Sir. Sorry. Can I get you something else?"

I sat and looked at the young man. He was smiling, doing the job he had been sort of trained for. It was a stepping-stone for him, hopefully before a life of university and a good job, somewhere, in a city. At that moment, though, he had no comprehension of what he had just said. How ridiculous it sounded. We had, basically, had four bottles of wine between us and he was now saying, as though it was normal, that they had none left. What sort of restaurant carried just four bottles of the grape stuff? I know it wasn't an end-of-the-world type of problem, but we were having a lovely time. The family was all together for the first time in a long time, and I just wanted another bottle so we could finish our evening on a high, and drunk.

"Can you pop out and get a couple at all?" I asked, genuinely. I could tell that the suggestion caused all sorts of confusement for our designated server, who made his excuses and scampered into the back.

We carried on, chatting away, and a couple of minutes later Tiny Tim, himself, approached us. He was well over 6ft tall and built like a brick shithouse. Confirmation, I suppose, that the restaurant was named for its size, not his. I explained the situation, calmly.

He peered at me.

"The shops are all closed, Sir, so I couldn't get you a bottle, even if I wanted to."

"Pubs are still open. I am sure they will let you have a couple," I countered.

"I'm not going into the pub to beg for some wine. Sorry. Let me just get your bill and let's call it a night, shall we?"

Tim then turned and disappeared, probably with the intention of returning with a card machine.

For some reason, this situation had begun to boil the proverbial. If he had just said he would try and get some, apologised for the situation, and offered this alternative, not the bill, I would have been fine. I was a stickler for customer service and this was not it. Wine was what I wanted now, and I was going to get it. The others were mostly oblivious to the shenanigans, still chatting away and laughing. I made an excuse that I needed some air and nipped out to one of the pubs, just yards opposite.

A couple of minutes later, I was back, armed with a cheap red and white that was pure extortion on the pub's part, but I didn't care. I was happy. I even had the foresight of getting them to open them with a corkscrew. No stone unturned in my quest to show Tiny Tim that the customer was always right and to go above and beyond in the name of service.

I started to pour the wine when Tim reappeared with his card machine. He didn't look a happy bunny as he arrived at our table and saw the wine flowing again.

"You can't drink that in here. You can take it away with you. Now, please."

His eyes peered deep into me again, quite unnervingly.

"I did give you the opportunity," I replied, smugly. "It was very easy to sort. We won't be long."

By now, the family had become aware of what was occurring. Dawn could see in my persona that I was having one of my stubborn moments when I am always right whatever the circumstances or consequences. Mum was still laughing, but she had already drunk more than normal so was a bit oblivious to the events. Craig and Jess were confused, still trying to work out what was happening.

"You leave me no choice then," Tim announced, before disappearing again.

There was then a period of calm. Nothing happened. Tim didn't come back. We carried on guzzling our naughty wine and I assumed that he had decided to just leave us to it, maybe bar me from ever visiting again, which was highly unlikely anyway.

Suddenly, we heard police sirens, then blue lights flashing through the drawn curtains.

"What the…?" Craig exclaimed, panicking. "They're not coming in here, are they?"

"Quite possibly," I replied, contemplating whether I should hide the two bottles of evidence under the table.

"You do know that Tiny Tim is a retired police detective?" queried Jess, looking slightly concerned.

No, I didn't, and it would have been helpful information well before that moment. I now understood his peering eyes.

The front entrance opened and in they came, the boys in blue. I counted five of them, calmly walking towards us which didn't take long at all. It was suddenly quite cramped and claustrophobic, to be honest. One of them was having a chat with Tim at the bar, pointing at me, whilst the others were nearly falling over our table due to the lack of space. I think Craig was trying to get under the darn thing, such was his embarrassment at the state of affairs.

"Craig?" said one of the officers, suddenly noticing him hiding behind a very small napkin.

"Hi, Bats," replied Craig. "You all right?"

"I'm great, thanks. What the heck is going on here?"

Bats, the policeman, had been childhood friends with Craig, the policeman. One had cleared off to Manchester to fight crime while the other, by the looks of it, had stayed local to raid tiny restaurants. Hopefully, good news for me though. They had a brief chat and then Bats wandered over to chat to Tim. After a couple of minutes, they were back, Tim by their side.

The atmosphere had changed in an instant. Suddenly they, and we, were all laughing, Tim and Craig were conversing as though they were long-lost mates. Bats was entertaining Charlotte with some magic tricks involving toothpicks, whilst Mum was just laughing at everything and anything.

Before I knew it, it had all been agreed amicably that we could finish his competitor's wine and take our time whilst doing it. The police left and, before long, it was as though nothing had happened. All very bizarre. Craig returned to conversations of days gone by with Mum, I was desperately removing the toothpicks from my daughter's grasp, whilst Dawn whispered 'knob' in my ear. Tim stood at the bar, by the front entrance, just smiling and nodding towards me.

Once we had settled up and left, we wandered through the lit, empty streets of the town. I smiled to myself as I passed the local pubs, the bakery café and newsagents. Nothing ever changes in a place like that. It made it both reassuring and frustrating, in equal measure. You could transport yourself back to when you were a teenager in an instant and the wonderful memories that went with it. But it also gave you a sense of relief, that you didn't have to walk past those buildings, day in, day out.

Craig was walking in front of us at speed, his bed crying out for him, as mine was for me. I jogged alongside him and put my arm around his shoulder.

"What on earth happened there?" I asked. "I thought we were going to get chucked out. Or worse."

"Nothing much. We stick together, that's all. An invisible code amongst us. Watch each other's backs, as long as it's not criminal, of course."

"Bit like our family then, I suppose," I said, squeezing his arm.

"Yeh, you're right, although there is always going to be the odd bad apple in any group or team. They usually disappear after a while or are told to leave."

He stopped and turned towards me. He smiled sadly before saying, "That was Dad in our case."

Chapter Thirteen:

There were a few fuzzy heads from the night before when we met at Mum's house, bright and early, the following morning. Dad's ashes were sitting upright, the cheap urn in the boot of my car housed by a Morrisons' carrier bag, which was rather fitting I thought. Thankfully, Bonnie had ignored the strange object in her space, which was rare. Normally, she would have torn the bag open and tried to open the metal object, hoping it would contain some tennis balls. Even she had sussed that this one should be left well alone.

The logistics and planning of Operation Ashes to Ashes wasn't my finest hour. We were all heading off in different directions after the event, so three cars were necessary to take Dad on his last journey. I was in the lead car as I was the only one who had the slightest idea where Ridge Rock was. Mum, Craig and Jess supported me in my desire to do the right thing which, whilst surprising, was much appreciated. I think they knew that it was the final closure and as such, for their own reasons, they wanted to be there.

We set off, heading towards the area I had identified. Charlotte, strapped in the back, was a bit crotchety from the night before and Dawn was already asleep. The weather was a mixed bag which was typical of the Yorkshire Dales. We had bright sunshine one minute, followed by a heavy shower the next. The gusts of wind decided to emerge and surprise you when you least expected it. I felt a slight void intensify in my heart as I kept tabs on the cars behind me through my rear-view mirror. This was to be the last act before our lives went back to normal. I realised that I would miss the time we had all spent together and miss the dad that I had got to know that previous week.

I took a turn to the left, off the main road and onto a single track that took us towards his final resting place. We were all in convoy, gently weaving our way up into the hills. The area was vast with just open fields, trees, and no passing places. This final part suddenly became a problem as we encountered a huge tractor coming the other way.

It was not a fair contest. One was designed for rough terrain, to plough through any ground. The other was a Mondeo, made for a travelling salesman on a motorway. There is, however, always a telepathic signal between drivers whenever this situation arises. One person decides to pull in, as far as possible, so allowing the other to pass. There is no faceoff, it just happens. The farmer was well on top of this arrangement and was in a deep trench on the right-hand side, a thin strip of tarmac in front of me. I gingerly made my way past, my wheels just avoiding the ditch on my left that was like a magnet to the eyes.

Mum was next, following me in her 4x4. She oozed confidence, with a look of impatience behind me. It was obvious that she was used to that manoeuvre, whilst my years away from this type of road had diminished my belief in that tight move. Bringing up the rear was Craig in his Renault Clio. I knew he would get through with no issues, being a fully-trained traffic cop. I was wrong. As we sat motionless in our cars, looking back, I could see the left side of his maroon car suddenly disappear from view. I waited to see if it would appear again, but no sign was forthcoming. I muttered under my breath and got out of the car, walking back to see what had happened.

I didn't laugh, but how I wanted to. The car was on an angle, with its two left wheels completely submerged. Even funnier, was the fact that Craig couldn't get out. He was so high up to the right that he had nowhere to go. His wife, Lisa, was also stuck as the passenger door was sandwiched on a bank of grass. He had a face like thunder, my smirk probably not helping his mood or the situation he was in.

The farmer had got out and was surveying the scene. He was shaking his head. I wasn't sure if that was because he was unsure how to help, or if he thought that my brother was an incompetent dickhead.

"Move your cars a bit further up," he bellowed to me in a contemptuous gruff voice. "Need some room to pull him out."

He meandered back to his tractor.

"Don't even think about trying to get out," he shouted back to the jammed car as he climbed back into his cab.

Craig had wound his window down and nodded in receipt of the blunt instructions. He was about to say something, but I think he realised that he was a bit goosed and that only Farmer Giles could save him. We did as were told and moved our cars further up the hill. I was praying that there wasn't going to be a further convoy of agricultural vehicles winging their way towards us as the tractor reversed, close to the bonnet of the Renault. I watched from afar, as the farmer hooked up a thick steel winch underneath the front of the car.

"When I put my thumbs up, I want you to put your foot on the accelerator."

He gave a thumbs-up as a reminder of his instructions.

"You got that?"

He didn't have many words but the ones he had were not wasted. Craig nodded and I swear he closed his eyes for a few seconds. The rescue team of one then fired up the tractor and began to move forward. The car started to dislodge slowly as the farmer put his thumbs up. Craig, who by then had reopened his eyes, revved loudly and the vehicle pulled away from the ditch. Lisa bounced back into her original seating position which was a sight to behold as her head wobbled from side to side. The important thing, though, was that the car was out and back on the road in one piece. Well, not quite.

As the tractor carried out its task, so the front bumper of Craig's beloved Clio separated from the rest of the vehicle. It was not a pretty sight. It was still attached, just, but half of it was flapping away in the wind. He was not a happy brother. The farmer, in contrast, was pleased with the result. That's what they always did in those circumstances. Just got you out. I think that he was secretly delighted with the damage. A timely reminder that we relocated city types shouldn't be anywhere near their stomping ground anymore.

"Sod this," Craig said angrily, as he got out of the car and stood looking at the damage. "Just drop the bloody ashes here. I need to get away. This needs fixing, pronto."

I understood his anger but that didn't stop my determination to finish what we had started. To find the right place, the elusive Ridge Rock.

"We are nearly there," I protested. "I am pretty sure it's just up here somewhere. We have come this far. Let's not give in now. You will regret it, I know you will."

Craig shook his head and got back in his car.

"Hurry up then," he shouted, his head popping out of his side window.

It would have been rather helpful if the rock which Dad wanted to be with had been signposted in some way. A nice plaque possibly, or a giant sign by the side of the road with an arrow pointing to the bloody thing. I had nothing like that to help me and, my God, there were hundreds of them in all shapes and sizes. We continued up the road slowly, looking right and left. For what? I hadn't a clue. Dawn, in the meantime, had gone back to sleep and was no help at all in the mission, whilst Charlotte kept pointing at the animals and shouting, "Moo".

At times, I thought we had gone too far and made the perilous decision of turning around and going back. That, of course, was potential vehicle suicide, but each time we all managed to navigate the tight turnaround without disappearing down a bank. Those never-ending manoeuvres didn't help Craig's mood one iota, his front bumper flapping away as he continued to follow wherever I went.

We stopped at certain times, got out of our cars and consulted, dodging the showers and swirling wind. Mum didn't say much, Jess just agreed with anything I suggested, whilst Craig kept saying he was definitely going home, only to get back in his car and follow me once again. He couldn't leave. None of us could. For some bizarre reason, we were all determined to finish it. Definitively.

It was about half an hour later, and having done at least four U-turns, that our collective patience ran out. Craig had been flashing his lights behind me, his arms waving furiously to pull over. I stopped and we reconvened in the middle of the road with hats and coats back on, protecting us from the elements.

"We can't keep doing this," Craig concluded, calmly. "We all want to do this, but let's face it, it is impossible."

He was right, sadly. I had, though, noticed one rock on our mini travels that kept catching my eye. It had a particular shape that, although not recognisable, was striking, tall and wide, that you could probably stand on or even sit. It was facing the town so I imagined you could look down and survey all the houses, shops and pubs. Although I had no idea if it was the elusive Ridge Rock, I did decide that it would suffice.

"Okay," I said, "follow me one last time, I think I know where we can do it."

A further half mile up the road, my chosen rock came back into view. We parked up, behind each other, still in a perfect convoy. I let Bonnie out of the boot and she was away, galloping through the heather and wildflowers. Dawn got Charlotte out, all wrapped up, and strapped her into the pushchair. The wind had disappeared but there was a constant drizzle, so we were all in our hats and coats with

Mum being the only one with the foresight to bring an umbrella.

I removed the urn, still in its Morrisons' bag, and trooped over to Craig.

"That rock is good enough for me," I said, pointing to the one I had noticed. "I think you should do the honours. Firstborn and all that. Stand on the top and make a little speech. Think that would be fitting, seeing as we have come this far."

I passed him the bag and then rested my hand on his shoulder.

Craig took the urn out of the bag and climbed onto the top of the rock. We all gathered around, the rain beginning to worsen and the cold starting to infiltrate our attire.

"Rest in peace, Dad," shouted Craig, as loud as he could. "I hope you will protect us in death, in a way you failed us in life."

Not quite the sermon I had envisaged.

He lifted the lid and began to shake the ashes out. Unfortunately, with spectacular timing, that was the moment the wind decided to return. It had also decided that it didn't fancy going in just one direction. A swirling one was required, just as Dad's dust was released.

This is another moment which is hard to describe and, blimey, there have been a few. His ashes blew all around us. The majority seemed to cover Craig, who was now screaming and frantically brushing his coat and hair with his

303

hands, but it also started to land on the tiny congregation down below, which included yours truly. As my mouth had automatically opened in shock at the unfolding events, so the dust entered it. I was spitting furiously, scraping my tongue with my fingers.

Looking around me, I stood traumatised. To my left, Bonnie was leaping in the air catching and swallowing fragments of Dad, having the time of her life. To my right, Mum seemed to be protected by the giant umbrella whilst Charlotte was giggling away, desperately trying to catch as many bits as possible, grabbing the black snow. Her pink Peppa Pig bobble hat was getting darker by the second and I suddenly realised that Dad would be visiting us after all. Meanwhile, Jess was the first to run for cover and the safety of a car.

We all started to follow her lead and run. The rain, wind, and ash blinded us as we followed her, trying to find a path to some protection. Dawn led the way, steering the pushchair like she was competing in some sort of parents' school race. Charlotte was bouncing up and down in the buggy, the giggles turning to tears as she felt every bump. I had managed to grab hold of Bonnie, her slavering chops still straining to catch any bit of my dad that she could. I looked behind me and caught sight of Craig sprinting as fast as he could, whilst Mum ambled, her trusty umbrella still doing its job.

Once we were back in our cars, we just sat, staring into nowhere. Dawn was far damper than me, having had the unenviable job of putting Charlotte back in the car. She was sat next to me, a few tell-tale embers still stuck on her cheeks. There was an expression of utter disbelief on her face. I peered into the back where Bonnie was panting in the boot, her pink tongue rather darker than usual. Charlotte was sat quietly, her thumb firmly embedded in her mouth, her bobble hat splattered in dark grey despite Dawn's best efforts to shake them off as she bundled her back in.

I looked through my rear-view mirror and could just make out Craig staring at me through his windscreen. I had no idea what state he was in and instinct told me not to go and find out. The rain was lashing down, the wind continuing to swirl violently. I knew that we wouldn't be getting out again, to discuss and dissect what had just occurred.

It was Craig who broke the static convoy first. Passing me as he set off, presumably for home, the front bumper still flapping, he gave me a hard stare as his car slowly proceeded past my window. They were quickly followed by Mum and Jess doing exactly the same thing, the two cars driving off into the distance, without an acknowledgement. Definitely no goodbye.

I took my coat off and threw it in the back. Not the wisest thing to do, as another flurry of ash landed on my arms, gear stick, and steering wheel. Dawn continued to look out of the window, avoiding any eye contact, her fingers concentrated on plucking any stray, damp, embers from her face. I started the ignition, gave a heavy sigh and, as the final vehicle still in place, started the long journey home.

Charlotte was fast asleep and, for once, Dawn was wide awake but in no mood for small talk. That was understandable in the circumstances. It did, though, give me plenty of time to mull over the previous week in my head. It had all been rather peculiar, to put it mildly.

Discovering the old money under the mattress and the witless disposal of it. The illogical, followed by mind-blowing, explanation with regards to the beneficiaries in his will. Miranda, the wonderful clairvoyant, who taught me to believe in the afterlife. The cremation, sponsored by Morrisons, and finally the debacle of my ridiculous decision to scatter his ashes in no man's land. In the middle of a monsoon.

As a family, we laugh about it now. At our rare get-togethers, that legendary week always comes up in our conversations. The stories have slightly changed over the years, and have been exaggerated dreadfully, but it is lovely and comforting. It's odd, but still sad, that I have very few memories from when Dad was alive, but so many through his demise. I will always remember him now, but only because of this one bizarre death.

Acknowledgements

There are, of course, one or two people I would like to thank for making this book possible.

Tom Cornwell for the cover design. He took my daft idea away and made it into something very special.

Christine Beech for proof reading and editing. Her instant understanding of my style and how I wanted it to flow was very helpful. The constant encouragement and constructive criticism improved me as a writer, and hopefully, made a better book.

Michael Heppell for his inspiration and enthusiasm. His Write That Book Masterclass, that my wife encouraged me to join, was fun, challenging, and inventive. Without him, I would never have even started, let alone finished the book.

Pete Metcalfe for finding me. As my former English teacher, we had lost touch for over 30 years when he got wind of what I was up to. Connecting with him was wonderful, and his instant passion and warmth for the book lifted my confidence when it had begun to waver.

The Yorkshire Dales for its beauty. The book is inspired by the people and surroundings of my early life there. It has brought back many fond memories of growing up in 'God's own country.'

Holly Mae Wilson for coming into my life. A daughter to be proud of, she has encouraged me from the start, always believed in me, and never mocked my desire to write.

Victoria Wilson-Crane for just being there. My wife and best friend, she inspired me to stop talking about it, and write the darn thing. A constant source of help and guidance, she listened patiently and with genuine excitement, to my ideas and progress. I am lucky to have her.

Finally, to Mary-Lou. I remember when we discussed writing a book, amongst so many topics, when we stayed up late into the night. This is for you.

Disclaimer

Some of the characters, stories, and events in this book are fictitious. Any similarity to real persons, living or dead, is coincidental and not intended by the author.

About The Author

Roger Wilson-Crane was born in Harpenden but raised in the idyllic Yorkshire Dales, which he hopes, makes him an honorary Yorkshireman.

His first foray into the world of writing was as a 14 year old when he wrote, directed, and performed a play for the school. Unfortunately, life and work interrupted this creativity and it didn't return until recently, when the desire resurfaced.

A keen amateur actor and singer, Roger has had the privilege of taking lead roles, across Yorkshire, in productions such as Guys and Dolls, Jesus Christ Superstar, and The Full Monty. The latter culminating in a NODA nomination for best actor.

A Managing Director of a successful private company in the Automotive sector, he made the decision to take a back seat from the business, in 2019, and concentrate on the writing passion still niggling away at him.

Roger lives in Doncaster, South Yorkshire with his wife Victoria, who inspires him every day. Their lives are never without a flat coat retriever in tow. The current one, Hastings, aged 5, a constant by their side. He has a 20 year old daughter, Holly Mae, who he is incredibly proud of and was the catalyst to finally become a published author.

Follow me on social media:

Website: www.rogerwilsoncrane.co.uk
Facebook: https://www.facebook.com/Certified2021
Twitter: https://twitter.com/certified2021
Instagram: https://www.instagram.com/rogerwilsoncrane/